Travel Guide to Ja

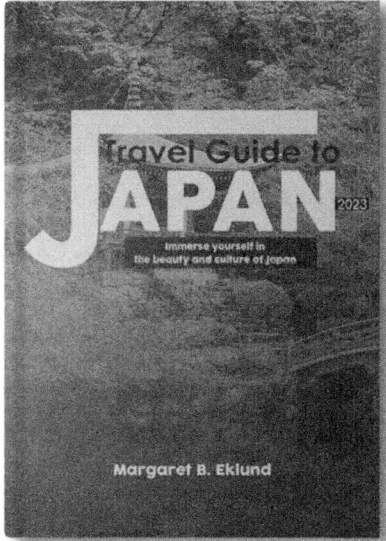

Immerse Yourself in the Beauty
and Culture of Japan

Margaret B. Eklund

1

Table of Contents

Introduction

Welcome to Japan, a fascinating nation where history and technology coexist together. Japan provides a broad selection of experiences that will leave you in amazement, from bustling cities to peaceful countryside. Japan has something to offer everyone, whether you are interested in history, food, or adventure.

This travel guide will help you navigate Japan's distinctive culture, traditions, and attractions as we take you on a tour of the country's top attractions. Learn about the dynamic city of Tokyo, which features tall buildings, hopping street markets, and top-notch cuisine. Immerse yourself in Kyoto's historic district, where exquisite temples and traditional Japanese architecture will take you back in time.

Discover Japan's natural beauties, from the recognizable Mount Fuji to the charming cherry blossom gardens. Traditional Japanese gardens and hot springs offer a calm escape, while hiking routes, ski slopes, and white-water rafting offer an exhilarating rural experience.

Enjoy a unique gastronomic experience while pampering your taste buds. Japan offers a wide variety of flavors that will tempt your tongue, from sushi and ramen to tempura and sake. Don't forget to try the local cuisine in each city you visit because every region has its distinctive culinary treats.

Throughout this book, we'll also give you useful details on getting about Japan, lodging possibilities, and pointers for managing its manners and traditions. This book will enable you to make the most of your time in Japan and develop lifelong memories, whether you are considering a brief visit or a longer stay.

Prepare to immerse yourself in Japan's rich culture and stunning scenery by packing your bags now.

Japan offers a voyage of discovery and awe, with its contemporary cities, exuberant festivals, and quiet gardens. Prepare to fall head over heels for the Land of the Rising Sun.

Overview of Japan

Japan is an island country in East Asia and is officially referred to as the Republic of Japan. Along with other smaller islands, it consists of four major islands: Honshu, Hokkaido, Kyushu, and Shikoku. It ranks as the tenth most populated nation in the world with a population of more than 125 million.

Japan has a long and rich history, as well as a strong cultural legacy. It was one of Asia's oldest civilizations to emerge, and its culture, art, religion, and philosophy still strongly affect those of the region today. For most of its history, the nation has been ruled by an emperor, but currently, the role is largely ceremonial.

One of the largest and most developed economies in the world is Japan. It is renowned for its technological advancements, top-notch manufacturing, and international exports. Some of the most well-known companies in the world are japanese such as Toyota, Honda, Sony, Nintendo, and Panasonic, canon, Toshiba, and. Sharp .

The prime minister serves as the head of government in Japan, which has a parliamentary constitutional monarchy system. The nation is renowned for its effective public transportation system, which includes the well-known Shinkansen bullet train, and for having a well-developed infrastructure.

The Japanese are renowned for their strict work ethic, politeness, and discipline. They place strong importance on respecting individuals as well as their environment. This is evident in the careful attention to detail they pay to a variety of facets of their lives, including traditional arts and crafts, tea rituals, and the idea of Omotenashi (hospitality).

Japan is well known for its distinctive and varied food. Sushi, ramen, tempura, and yakitori are examples of traditional Japanese cuisine or Washoku. Additionally, the nation is well-known for its matcha (powdered green tea) and sake (rice wine).

Millions of tourists visit Japan each year to discover its historical monuments, breathtaking natural landscapes, and energetic cities. Popular tourist sites include Mount Fuji, the iconic volcano that is regarded as a symbol of the nation, Kyoto, the cultural and historical center of Japan, and Tokyo, the capital city, which is noted for its modernity and energetic environment.

Additionally well-known is Japan's distinctive pop culture, which has become increasingly well-liked abroad. Japanese pop music, manga (Japanese comic books), and anime have attracted audiences all over the world. The nation holds festivals and events all year long, such as cherry blossom viewing in the spring, exciting festivals in the summer, and the fall leaf season.

Despite its modernity, Japan has a strong bond with the natural world. The nation is renowned for its breathtaking national parks, onsen hot springs, and gardens. Numerous outdoor pursuits are available, including hiking, skiing, and exploring the area's many beautiful paths.

But Japan too has to deal with some difficulties. Natural calamities including typhoons, earthquakes, and tsunamis are common there. Other problems the nation faces include an aging population and a declining birth rate, which have an impact on both the economy and society.

In conclusion, Japan is a fascinating nation with a special fusion of traditional culture and contemporary innovation. Travelers from all over the world find it to be an intriguing destination because of its fascinating history, rich cultural heritage, cutting-edge technology, and breathtaking landscapes.

Making Travel Plans for Japan

Japan is an intriguing nation with a rich cultural heritage and beautiful natural surroundings. Japan has something to offer everyone, whether they want to visit historic temples, take in the bustle of contemporary city life, or simply unwind in hot springs. However, because of the language barrier and the wide range of attractions, organizing a vacation to Japan can be quite difficult. Here are some suggestions to aid with vacation preparation and help you make the most of your time in Japan.

1. Determine Your Vacation's Length: The first stage in organizing your vacation to Japan is determining how long you intend to spend there. Even though Japan is a small country, there is a lot to see and do there. To see all the key attractions, you should ideally plan on staying at least two weeks. If you just have a limited amount of time,

prioritize your travel destinations and make your plans appropriately.

2. Establish Your Budget: Traveling to Japan may be expensive, particularly in large cities like Tokyo and Kyoto. Establish your spending limit and schedule your lodging, travel, and activities accordingly. To save money, think about staying in guest houses or hostels or using the public transportation system instead of a taxi.

3. Pick the Right Time to Visit: There are four distinct seasons in Japan, and each has its allure. It's beautiful to see the cherry blossoms in the spring, the vivid fall foliage, and the snowy vistas in the winter. When deciding when to visit, take the weather and the things you wish to do into account. Plan carefully because major tourist spots may become congested during the high season.

4. Do Your Research and Plan Your Itinerary: There are many attractions in Japan, including historical

landmarks, cutting-edge cities, and natural wonders. Depending on your interests, research the must-see locations, and plan a schedule that gives you ample time to explore each area. Make sure to balance well-known attractions with off-the-beaten-path locations and cultural experiences.

5. Recognize Your Options: Japan boasts a first-rate, highly effective, and interconnected public transportation system. Between major cities, the Shinkansen (bullet train) is a well-liked and practical mode of transportation. Think about getting a Japan Rail Pass, which can help you save money and gives you unrestricted access to JR trains. To navigate cities, you should also become familiar with local transportation choices like buses and subways.

6. Learn a Few Basic Japanese Phrases: While English is widely spoken in popular tourist destinations, learning a few fundamental Japanese phrases will help you get around the nation and

communicate with locals. Learning to say hello, thank you, please, and excuse me will help you to be respectful and polite. Apps and phrasebooks are helpful learning tools for fundamental phrases.

7. Take into account Cultural Etiquette: Before going, you should be informed of the peculiar customs and etiquette of Japan. For instance, removing your shoes before entering a home or other traditional building, bowing to show respect, and using chopsticks properly. To respect and accept the regional customs, learn about and adhere to these cultural practices.

8. Sample Local Cuisine: Local cuisine is a must-try while visiting Japan because it is so well-known throughout the world. There are countless possibilities, from tempura and yakitori to ramen and sushi. Be daring and experiment with new tastes and specialties. Remember to say "Itadakimasu" before a meal and "Gochisousama Deshita" after you've finished showing appreciation,

as well as other customs related to dining in the area.

9. Pack appropriately: The climate in Japan varies, so bring clothing that will work for the conditions there. You'll probably be doing a lot of walking, so you must have comfortable walking shoes. Don't forget to bring any necessary medications, as well as any electronic adapters.

10. Become familiar with safety precautions: Although Japan is typically a safe country, it is always advisable to be aware of safety measures. Take the required security measures to protect your things, observe traffic laws when crossing streets, and avoid going for a nighttime stroll alone in uncharted territory. A wise option is to purchase travel insurance to protect against any unforeseen events.

11. Purchase travel insurance: Even though it's crucial to travel safely, unforeseen events might still

occur. It makes sense to purchase travel insurance that provides coverage for lost luggage, trip cancellations, and medical emergencies. Make sure you have sufficient coverage for your vacation by checking with your insurance provider.

12. Maintain Connectivity: Maintaining a connection when traveling is crucial for communication, navigation, and emergencies To have internet connectivity on your trip, think about renting a pocket Wi-Fi or getting a SIM card for your phone. You will be able to stay in touch with friends and family, use navigation apps, and translate menus thanks to this.

You can arrange a memorable and enjoyable trip to Japan by paying attention to these suggestions. Be sure to immerse yourself in the fascinating culture and breathtaking sights that the nation has to offer, and keep an open mind about your plans in case something unexpected comes up. Traveling to Japan will leave you with enduring memories. You can perhaps use this guide to organize your trip to Japan!

Ideal Season to Visit Japan

Beautiful Japan has a lot to offer tourists in the way of attractions and things to do. The ideal time to visit Japan, however, may vary depending on your travel goals and personal tastes. When organizing your visit, keep the following things in mind:

1. Cherry Blossom Season (Late March to Early April): The cherry blossom season, when the nation is covered in stunning pink and white blooms, is one of Japan's most recognizable seasons. Even though it's a popular time to go, it might get busy. Although the precise timing can vary from year to year, the blooms normally reach their peak in Tokyo and other large cities in late March or early April.

2. fall (Late September to Early December): The changing of the leaves into vibrant shades of red,

orange, and yellow throughout the fall season is another popular time to visit Japan. Some of the best locations to view the fall leaves include Hokkaido, Kyoto, and Nikko. Since the weather is typically moderate during this time, outdoor activities and sightseeing are appropriate.

3. Winter (December to February): Traveling to Japan in the winter is a fantastic option if you want to ski or snowboard. Popular ski areas with great snow conditions and amenities include Niseko, Hakuba, and Shiga Kogen. Winter is also a great time to indulge in wonderful winter fare like hot pots and ramen as well as relax in hot springs (onsen).

4. Spring and Fall (Mid-April to May and October to November): Visiting Japan in the spring or fall is a wonderful choice if you enjoy moderate weather and fewer tourists. These are the best times to visit the nation's stunning gardens, temples, and shrines

because the weather is more pleasant. Additionally, it's a terrific season for outdoor pursuits like hiking.

5. Summer (June to August): The summers in Japan, particularly in Tokyo and other urban regions, can be hot and muggy. However, the summer months can be more pleasant if you intend to travel to Hokkaido or mountainous areas. Summer is a fantastic time to participate in festivals (matsuri) and take part in seasonal events like fireworks displays and summer festivals.

6. Avoid Golden Week: From the end of April until the beginning of May, several national holidays are observed as "Golden Week." Since many Japanese people are on vacation around this period, there will be crowds of tourists and higher hotel rates. It is better to stay away from Japan during this time if at all feasible.

The best time to visit Japan will depend on your particular choices and the experiences you hope to have there, in sum. Japan has something to offer for every season, whether you want to see the breathtaking cherry blossoms, engage in outdoor activities in the fall, indulge in winter sports, or discover the local festivities. When organizing your trip to Japan, take into account the weather, the amount of traffic, and the exact activities you wish to partake in. It's also crucial to take into account the existing travel restrictions, the weather, and any festivals or events taking place at the time of your planned visit. For a memorable and enjoyable vacation to Japan, do your research and make the necessary plans.

Entry Requirements and visas

1. Passport: All visitors must have a passport that is current and has at least six months left on it after the date of admission. At least two blank pages in the passport are required for stamping.

2. Visa: Depending on the country of citizenship, different visas are needed. While some nations may

qualify for visa-free travel or visa on arrival, others could need a visa to enter. For precise visa needs, it is advised to contact the nearest embassy or consulate.

3. Visa-Free Travel: For a brief time, generally for travel or business, citizens of some nations are permitted to enter without a visa. The maximum amount of time you can stay without a visa varies, typically falling between 30 and 90 days. It is crucial to remember that visa-free access may not allow for working or studying in the nation.

4. Visa on Arrival: For some nationalities, some nations provide a visa-on-arrival option. This implies that visitors can seek a visa at the airport or land border upon arrival. The tourist must fulfill certain requirements and pay a fee to obtain a visa on arrival, which is typically valid for a set period.

5. Electronic Travel Authorization (ETA) systems have been implemented in some nations for

particular nationalities. This means that before a trip, tourists must submit an online ETA application. Depending on the country's policy, the ETA allows for visa-free entrance or visa on arrival and is electronically connected to the passport.

6. Reason for Visit: Visitors should be ready to present proof of the reason for their trip, such as hotel reservations, round-trip airline tickets, invitation letters, or evidence of sufficient funds to cover their expenses.

7. immunizations: Particularly for diseases that are common in the area, certain nations may require travelers to receive specific immunizations before admission. It is advisable to research the destination country's immunization regulations and advice before departure.

8. COVID-19 Testing and Quarantine: As a result of the current COVID-19 pandemic, many nations have added further entrance criteria, such as

obligatory COVID-19 testing before arrival, obligatory quarantine periods after arrival, or documentation of immunization. It's crucial to be informed about the most recent COVID-19-related requirements and travel cautions.

9. extra criteria: Depending on the country of destination, passengers may be subject to extra criteria, such as a thorough travel plan, proof of travel insurance, or financial stability. Before departing, it is a good idea to check the nation's precise admission criteria.

To ensure compliance with the laws of the target country, visitors must check the visa and entry requirements well in advance of their journey. Entry may be denied or there may be delays at the border if the prerequisites are not met. For the most recent and correct information on visa and entry requirements, it is advised to contact the relevant embassy or consulate.

Transportation in Japan

One of the most cutting-edge and effective transportation networks in the world is found in Japan. Here are a few of the primary transportation options in Japan:

1. Trains: The backbone of Japan's transportation system is the country's massive train network. The Shinkansen, or bullet train, connects major cities throughout the nation and is renowned for its quickness and punctuality. Japan boasts a vast network of local and regional trains in addition to the Shinkansen, making it simple to reach even the most isolated locations.

2. metro: The metro systems in Japan's major cities, such as Tokyo, Osaka, and Kyoto, are extensive, effective, and simple to use. The subway systems in the cities are well-connected and provide a practical means of transportation.

3. Buses: Buses are a well-liked option for traveling small distances, particularly in rural locations where

there may not be as many train options. The country's biggest cities are connected by long-distance buses as an alternative to trains.

4. Taxis: Taxis are easily accessible in cities and can be obtained at designated taxi stands or flagged down on the street. Compared to other modes of transportation, taxis in Japan are recognized for being quite pricey but also for being clean and professional.

5. Renting a car is a practical choice for visiting rural areas or seeing Japan's most isolated regions. However, driving in big cities might be difficult because of the congested traffic and high parking costs. It's crucial to remember that people in Japan drive on the left side of the road.

6. Bicycle: Thanks to the country's extensive network of bike lanes, bicycles are a common form of short-distance transportation in many Japanese cities. Numerous locations provide bike rental

services, and cycling is a fantastic way to discover the city's districts and attractions.

7. Ferries: Because Japan is an archipelago with several islands, ferries play a significant role in inter-island transit. Travelers frequently use ferries to get to places like Okinawa, Hokkaido, and the Seto Inland Sea.

8. Air travel: Within Japan, longer trips are frequently made by domestic flight. Flying can be a time-saving choice for traveling between far-flung places because Japan has a number of significant airports.

It is important to note that Japan has a very effective and dependable transportation infrastructure that makes it simple for locals and visitors to see the nation. Tourists can purchase the Japan Rail Pass, which provides unlimited travel on most trains for a certain length of time at a reasonable price, making it an affordable choice for seeing the country.In conclusion, Japan provides a variety of transportation choices to meet the demands of every traveler. Japan's transportation network is well-developed, dependable, and practical, with high-speed bullet trains, effective subway systems, buses, taxis, rental cars, bicycles, ferries, and domestic aircraft among its many modes of transportation. There are many ways to get around and explore everything Japan has to offer, whether you're traveling through cities, rural areas, or far-flung islands.Japan stresses accessibility by making sure that everyone can use their transportation systems. Elevators, escalators, and platforms with gap fillers are common in train stations and subway systems for convenient boarding. Individuals with impairments can ride on buses and cabs as well. Japan is always attempting to increase transportation accessibility, making it a friendly destination for all tourists.To be aware of regarding Japanese transportation:

1. Japan's transportation system is based mostly on trains, with the Shinkansen serving as the most well-known and effective means of transportation between major cities.

2. It is simple to move around in cities like Tokyo, Osaka, and Kyoto thanks to their efficient and extensive subway systems.

3. Buses are a well-liked means of transportation, particularly in rural locations where there may be minimal train service.

4. Although they can be pricey in comparison to other forms of transportation, taxis are widely available in cities.

5. Renting a car is a practical way to explore rural areas, while it can be difficult to drive in big towns.

6. Many cities have specialized infrastructure for cycling, making bicycles a common means of transportation for short distances.

7. Ferries are necessary for getting around islands.

8. For longer distances within the nation, domestic air travel offers a time-saving alternative.

Japan's public transportation system is renowned for being effective, hygienic, and simple to use. In addition, initiatives are taken to provide accessibility for those with impairments, making it a welcome location for all tourists.

Language and Communication

Japanese language and communication patterns have been greatly influenced by the country's lengthy and complex history. Japanese has a distinctive writing system that combines two phonetic scripts called Hiragana and Katakana with Chinese-inspired Kanji characters. The blend of writing systems gives the Japanese a unique appearance and feel.

Japanese speakers are renowned for their indirectness and politeness when speaking. Different social circumstances call for varying degrees of formality and politeness. For instance, you can address someone differently depending on their age, status, and relationship with you. To appreciate someone with a higher social rank, particular honorific and modest speech styles are also used.

In Japanese culture, nonverbal communication is also significant. The length and intensity of a bow can change depending on the circumstance.Bowing is a customary greeting and show of respect in Japan.The depth and the duration of bow can convey various meaning.Eye contact is typically anticipated and regarded as a sign of respect and focus. Direct eye contact can, however, also be interpreted in some situations as being forceful or confrontational.

Japan is renowned for its high-context communication style in addition to spoken and nonverbal communication. This means that when talking in Japan, it's critical to pay attention to context, body language, and tone as a lot of meaning is communicated through subtle indications and shared cultural understandings. Communication between Japanese people is typically more restrained and amicable, stressing cooperation and avoiding conflict.

In Japanese culture, there is a strong emphasis on indirect and ambiguous communication because group harmony is highly valued. Japanese people frequently utilize euphemisms or communicate in indirect ways to avoid upsetting or upsetting others. Because of this, it can occasionally be difficult for visitors to grasp the entire significance of what is being conveyed.

In Japanese communication, establishing and sustaining positive relationships is extremely crucial. Before getting into business topics, there is a great emphasis on developing trust and rapport. It is common for small chats and socializing to be viewed as crucial preludes to doing business, and it is expected that you will take the time to get to know each other personally.

Japan has recently shown a growing interest in English and Western culture. Many Japanese individuals, particularly younger generations, have a basic understanding of the language thanks to the widespread teaching of English in schools nowadays. However, English proficiency is still lacking, particularly in more rural places. Therefore, improving communication and developing connections in Japan can be greatly aided by having a basic understanding of Japanese customs and expressions. Overall, cultural values like politeness, indirectness, harmony, and the value of forming connections have a significant impact on language and communication in Japan. Understanding and observing these cultural conventions can substantially improve communication in Japan. The distinctive cultural traditions of Japan have a significant impact on the country's language and communication. Japanese is a difficult language to learn since it has three different writing systems: Katakana, another phonetic writing system, is used for onomatopoeia and foreign words, while

Hiragana is used for words that are native to Japan and employs Chinese characters. The unique structure and appearance of the Japanese are a result of this blending of writing systems.

It's common knowledge that Japanese communication is indirect and polite. To avoid open conflict or offending, Japanese people frequently utilize euphemisms and implicit language to express their thoughts and sentiments. Foreigners may occasionally find it challenging to comprehend this indirect communication style because the genuine meaning is frequently concealed beneath the surface.

Nonverbal cues are just as significant in Japanese communication as verbal cues are. A common greeting and way to express respect is to bow, with the length and intensity of the bow signifying the degree of respect. Generally, eye contact is kept during a conversation, yet excessive or prolonged eye contact might be considered rude. Additionally crucial in expressing emotions and intentions are body language and facial expressions.

The idea of "wa," which stands for harmony and social cohesiveness, permeates Japanese communication. A lot of emphasis is placed on upholding goodwill and averting confrontation. As a result, Japanese people appreciate consensus and give collective requirements precedence over personal preferences. This can occasionally result in a preference for reaching agreements and making decisions through talks in groups.

Japanese communication likewise emphasizes hierarchy and deference to authority. In formal contexts, it is customary to address those who are older or more respected with honorific words. The degree of formality and courtesy in language can change based on the social setting and the relationships between people.

The desire to learn English and adopt Western communication practices has grown in Japan in recent years. Since English is taught in schools, a lot of young Japanese people are familiar with its fundamentals. However, English proficiency is still scarce, particularly outside of big cities. It can be helpful to have a basic understanding of Japanese words and habits to communicate with natives.

Overall, social standards and cultural traditions are strongly ingrained in Japanese language and communication. Communication and relationship-building in Japan can be substantially improved by comprehending and respecting these practices.

Currency and Payment Methods

The Japanese yen (JPY) is the currency used in Japan. All domestic transactions are conducted in yen, which is the nation's official currency. Coins are available in the following denominations: 1 yen, 5 yen, 10 yen, 50 yen, 100 yen, and 500 yen. Banknotes are available in the following denominations: 1,000 yen, 2,000 yen, 5,000 yen, and 10,000 yen.

Paying Procedures:

1. Cash: In Japan, cash is commonly used and accepted. It is advised to always have some cash on hand because some locations might not accept cards.

2. Credit and Debit Cards: In Japan, especially in urban areas, credit and debit cards are commonly accepted. Commonly used credit cards include Visa, Mastercard, American Express, and JCB. It is significant to remember that certain shops, particularly smaller local ones, do not accept foreign credit cards.

3. Mobile Payments: In recent years, mobile payment methods have grown in popularity. Users are able to make contactless payments using their cellphones thanks to services like Apple Pay, Google Pay, and Suica (an IC card connected to mobile devices).

4. IC Cards: Rechargeable smartcards like Suica, Pasmo, and Icoca can be used to make small purchases at convenience stores, vending machines, and select restaurants in addition to using public transportation.

5. Electronic Money: Rakuten Pay, PayPay, and Line Pay are a few examples of the electronic money services that are commonly utilized in Japan. Through these services, customers can add money to their accounts and pay participating merchants with their mobile devices or specialty cards.

6. Bank Transfers: For major transactions, such paying rent or utility bills, bank transfers or wire transfers are frequently used. Instead of everyday purchases, this strategy is often utilized for domestic transactions.

7. Traveler's Cheques: Although previously a popular means of payment for travellers, traveler's

cheques are now less frequently used. Traveler's checks might not be accepted by many businesses, therefore it might be more convenient to use another form of payment.

Although Japan is generally a cash-based country, electronic payment options are becoming more common, especially in major cities and popular tourist destinations. To have a comfortable payment experience in Japan, it is advised to have a combination of cash and cards or electronic payment alternatives

Safety and Security Tips

1. Obey local laws and ordinances: Get to know Japan-specific laws and ordinances, such as those pertaining to public transit, cultural norms, and traffic. Your safety and security will be enhanced if you abide by these guidelines.

2. Be aware of your surroundings: Be mindful of your surroundings, particularly while in busy places, popular destinations, or on public transit.

Always keep an eye on your stuff and be on the lookout for pickpockets.

3. Monitor weather developments: Typhoons, earthquakes, and significant snowfall are common in Japan. Keep abreast of the weather and heed any directions or cautions issued by local authorities.

4. Always carry identification with you: Bring a passport or a copy of your visa if you need to prove your identity. This will be crucial if there is a disaster or if you have to present identification to the police.

5. Take safety measures against environmental dangers: volcanic eruptions and earthquake activity are common in Japan. Learn the proper safety precautions to follow in the event of an earthquake or volcanic eruption, and be aware of where the nearest emergency shelters are located.

6. Exercise caution when consuming alcohol: People frequently drink in public in Japan due to the country's strong drinking culture. On the other hand, binge drinking may provide safety risks. Be cautious when drinking and be alert of your surroundings, particularly if you're out alone at night.

7. Protect your possessions: Ensure the safety of your possessions, particularly priceless papers, cash, and technology. When available, use the hotel safes or lockers; keep valuables hidden from view.

8. Be on the lookout for frauds: Like any well-known tourist location, there might be scammers that prey on unwary tourists. Be wary of anyone attempting to assist you excessively, offering their services without your permission, or requesting money or personal information. When making reservations, use trusted websites and refrain from giving out personal information to unauthorized people or websites.

9. Become familiar with emergency phone numbers: Confirm that you are aware of the police, ambulance, and fire emergency numbers in your area. Knowing the location of the closest police station, hospital, and embassy or consulate is also useful.

10. Respect regional traditions and customs: Because Japan has such a rich cultural legacy, it is crucial to respect and uphold regional traditions and customs. To demonstrate respect and prevent any misunderstandings or inadvertent offense, be aware of basic etiquette and educate yourself on things like bowing and taking off your shoes in specific locations.

11. Travel safely: Japan boasts a first-rate public transportation network that includes trains, buses, and the metro. However, be wary of the crowds during rush hour and stay alert to any dangers like pickpocketing. When using public transportation,

abide by the safety regulations and make sure you have the knowledge and tools required to operate the system.

12. Prevent natural catastrophes by taking the necessary preparations and becoming familiar with the emergency protocols for earthquakes, tsunamis, and other natural disasters. Pay attention to warnings and heed local authorities' directions. Locate a safe area in the event of an emergency, and keep yourself updated with local news and emergency notifications.

13. Always have emergency supplies on hand: It's a good idea to have a basic emergency kit that contains necessities like water, non-perishable food, flashlights, batteries, a first aid kit, and any necessary prescriptions. This will ensure that you are ready in the event of an emergency or natural disaster.

14. Exercise caution when making loud noises: Japan places a high importance on peace and harmony, thus making loud noises could be seen as rude. Pay attention to the noise levels, especially in populated regions, lodgings, and public places. Avoid having loud talks, turning up the music, or acting in a disruptive way that can cause trouble.

15. Follow your instincts: If something feels off or uncomfortable, follow your instincts and leave the area or call for help. It's always preferable to.

Information on Health and Medicine

1. Healthcare System: The National Health Insurance (NHI), a nationwide healthcare program in Japan, is financed by a combination of employee and employer payments. It is one of the best healthcare systems in the world and offers complete coverage to all inhabitants of Japan.

2. Hospitals: There are numerous public and private hospitals in Japan. Private hospitals are smaller and

more specialized, whereas public hospitals are often bigger and situated in cities. Tokyo General Hospital, St. Luke's International Hospital, and Osaka University Hospital are a few of the well-known hospitals in Japan.

3. Doctors and Specialists: With a high doctor-to-population ratio, Japan offers its citizens access to a wide spectrum of medical specialists. "House doctors" are primary care physicians who can refer patients to specialists when necessary. Internal medicine, pediatrics, obstetrics & gynecology, orthopedics, and dermatology are a few common medical specializations.

4. Health Insurance: Everyone who lives in Japan must have health insurance. The majority of people are insured by the National Health Insurance, however, most employees also have access to their employer's Employee's Health Insurance. The government's Health and Welfare Services for the Uninsured provide coverage for those without

insurance. In most cases, the patient and the insurance company split the cost of healthcare, with the patient bearing some of the financial burden.

5. Medical Examinations: Japan places a high priority on preventative healthcare and provides routine medical examinations for citizens. The local government often offers these examinations at a discounted or free price. To identify and prevent any health problems, the check-ups involve a variety of testing, including blood pressure, cholesterol, and cancer screenings.

6. Medical Tourism: Patients from all over the world seeking specialist medical treatments or procedures flock to Japan, a popular destination for medical tourism. The nation is recognized for its cutting-edge medical equipment and highly qualified medical personnel. Medical tourists frequently seek out cosmetic surgery, orthopedic procedures, and cutting-edge cancer therapies.

7. Conventional Western medicine is not the only form of medicine practiced in Japan; Kampo, or traditional medicine, has a long history there. In Japan, a type of herbal medicine known as Kampo has been used for centuries. A lot of hospitals and clinics in Japan provide integrated healthcare that combines Western and traditional Japanese medicine.

8. Emergency Services: Japan has a sophisticated emergency medical infrastructure. Calling the emergency hotline number, 119, will put you in touch with an ambulance service that will take you to the closest suitable hospital. Japan's emergency medical services are quite effective and prepared to deal with a variety of emergencies.

9. Pharmacies: There are pharmacies in nearly every neighborhood in Japan. Along with prescription medicines, they offer a huge selection of OTC meds. It is crucial to remember that while some

medications can be bought without a prescription from a doctor, others must.

10. Health and Safety Advice: When traveling to Japan, it is advised to have travel insurance that covers medical expenses. It's also crucial to be informed about any health or travel recommendations that the government may issue. To interact effectively with healthcare practitioners, it's also a good idea to have a basic familiarity with Japanese medical and healthcare jargon. Finally, maintaining excellent hygiene by routinely washing your hands and receiving the required vaccinations will help stop the spread of disease.

Travel Protection

Although visiting another country can be an exciting and rewarding experience, it's necessary to be ready for any unforeseen circumstances that can arise. Travel insurance can help with that. While you tour the lovely nation of Japan, you may have peace of mind knowing that travel insurance provides safety and coverage for a range of situations.

Following are some characteristics and advantages of travel insurance in Japan:

1. Medical coverage: Travel insurance covers any unanticipated medical costs that may occur while you are traveling. This covers any necessary emergency medical care, hospitalization, and evacuation. The high-quality healthcare system in Japan makes it crucial to have sufficient coverage in case of medical crises.

2. vacation interruption or cancellation: Unexpected circumstances occasionally may compel you to postpone or cancel your vacation. Your non-refundable charges, such as airfare, lodging, and activities that you have already paid for, may be covered by travel insurance. Having this coverage is usually a smart idea, especially for journeys lasting a long time or entailing substantial outlays.

3. Baggage and personal items: Loss, theft, or damage to your luggage and personal items is also covered by travel insurance. Travel insurance can assist in reimbursing you for the value of your lost belongings if your luggage is misplaced by an airline or stolen while you are traveling. This insurance guarantees that you may replace your necessities and continue your journey without incurring any additional costs.

4. Travel delays: Travel insurance covers any costs incurred as a result of missed connections or delays in transportation. Travel insurance can cover any additional lodging, food, and transportation costs you might spend as a result of a delayed or canceled flight.

5. Personal liability: Travel insurance offers coverage for any monetary damages or legal costs you might incur if you accidentally cause harm to a third party. This insurance makes sure that you are

safeguarded in the event of any unanticipated mishaps or occurrences while on your trip.

It's crucial to remember that the coverage amounts, exclusions, and costs of travel insurance policies might vary. Before acquiring travel insurance, it is advised to thoroughly study the policy documentation and comprehend the terms and circumstances. Additionally, contrast many insurance companies to discover the finest coverage at the lowest cost.

Travel insurance is a crucial investment in your safety and wellbeing when visiting Japan. It makes sure you may enjoy your trip to the fullest without being concerned that unplanned circumstances would ruin your plans. Therefore, to travel to Japan without stress and enjoy yourself, make sure to purchase travel insurance before you leave.

Introduction to Tokyo

Tokyo, the vibrant capital city of Japan, is well-known for its distinctive fusion of tradition and modernity. Tokyo, one of the world's most populous cities, provides visitors with exceptional and life-changing experiences. This vibrant city has much to offer everyone, from its renowned skyscrapers and neon-lit streets to its ancient temples and peaceful gardens. Tokyo is sure to make an impression, whether you want to explore the various neighborhoods, indulge in the top-notch cuisine, or fully immerse yourself in the fascinating culture and history. Pack your luggage and prepare to explore Tokyo's treasures, where the past and future collide in fascinating ways. The intriguing destination of Tokyo, the nation's capital, is a prime example of how tradition and innovation can coexist in perfect harmony. This vibrant city is a fusion of historic temples, cutting-edge skyscrapers, lively street markets, and tranquil gardens. The city offers a wide variety of activities to suit all interests, from the famed Tsukiji Fish Market to the iconic Tokyo Tower. Tokyo is a city that skillfully blends efficiency and elegance thanks to its first-rate infrastructure, effective public transit system, and friendly people. Tokyo is a compelling city that will captivate you at every turn, whether you wish to explore the historical landmarks, indulge in the local cuisine, or simply immerse yourself in the bustling atmosphere. Tokyo, Japan's throbbing capital, is a dynamic metropolis that skillfully combines tradition and innovation. Tokyo is a unique city with its tall skyscrapers, busy streets, and top-notch cuisine. Tokyo offers a distinctive experience that appeals to all interests, from tranquil gardens and ancient temples to cutting-edge technology and fashionable clothing. Tokyo has much to offer everyone, whether you enjoy history, gastronomy, shopping, or the arts. So come and experience Tokyo's lively energy firsthand while learning about its beauty. Japan's enormous metropolis, Tokyo, is a city where traditional culture and cutting-edge technology coexist in perfect harmony. Tokyo is a city that never fails to enthrall visitors with its tall skyscrapers, busy streets, and colorful culture. Tokyo offers a wide variety of experiences for all types of travelers, from its world-class retail areas like Ginza and Harajuku to its tranquil parks and temples like Meiji Shrine and Senso-ji. There is no shortage of adventure in this vibrant city, whether you want to experience real sushi at a neighborhood izakaya, get lost in the vibrant world of anime and manga, or just take in the stunning views from the Tokyo Skytree. Prepare to get lost in Tokyo's neon wonders and cultural treasures as you learn why it's regarded as one of the most interesting cities in the world.

Top Attractions in Tokyo

1. Tokyo Disneyland - One of the city's most visited attractions, Tokyo Disneyland delivers a fantastic experience with its fantasy-themed zones,

exhilarating rides, fun shows, and lovable Disney characters.

2. Tokyo Tower - With a height of 333 meters, the Tokyo Tower is a well-known representation of the city. From its observation decks, visitors may take in expansive views of Tokyo; they can also visit the aquarium and eat at the tower's restaurants.

3. Sens-ji Temple – The oldest temple in Tokyo, Sens-ji is a must-see destination. Visitors can take in the temple's beautiful architecture, the bustling Nakamise shopping district, and traditional Japanese culture.

4. Meiji Shrine - Emperor Meiji and Empress Shoken are honored at the Meiji Shrine, which is situated in the center of Tokyo. Visitors can wander peacefully around the grounds' forests, partake in customary Shinto ceremonies, and take in the beautiful ambiance.

5. Tsukiji Fish Market - One of the biggest fish markets in the world, Tsukiji Fish Market is a culinary lover's dream. Visitors can enjoy mouthwatering sushi, watch the lively auction of fresh seafood, and browse the colorful market stalls.

6. Shinjuku Gyoen National Garden - This vast garden offers a tranquil retreat from Tokyo's bustle. During the spring, visitors can take in the stunning scenery, wander among the numerous gardens, and enjoy a picnic beneath cherry blossom trees.

7. Akihabara - Known as the center of Japanese pop culture and electronics, Akihabara is a bustling neighborhood dotted with electronics shops, arcades for playing video games, and shops selling anime. Visitors can experience the distinctive Otaku culture firsthand and shop for the newest technology.

8. Ueno Park - Ueno Park is a sizable park that combines cultural and ecological elements. The Tokyo National Museum, the Ueno Zoo, and other

museums are open to visitors, who may also enjoy picnicking by the park's tranquil pond and viewing cherry blossom trees in the spring.

9. Odaiba - This man-made island in Tokyo Bay is renowned for its cutting-edge structures, malls, and entertainment venues. Visitors can unwind at the beach, explore the well-known Odaiba Palette Town, and take in the breathtaking city views from the waterfront.

10. Shibuya Crossing - One of Tokyo's most recognizable landmarks, Shibuya Crossing is known for its pedestrian scramble. Visitors can explore the bustling commercial and entertainment sector as well as witness the organized chaos of people crossing the street from different directions.

11. Tokyo Skytree - Tokyo Skytree is the tallest tower in Japan, rising to a height of 634 meters. From its observation decks, visitors may take in breathtaking views of the city, shop for trinkets, and eat at the tower's restaurants.

12. Ginza - One of Tokyo's most opulent retail areas, Ginza features a large selection of upmarket shops, department stores, and eateries. Indulge in fine dining, watch a performance at the Kabuki-za theater, and shop for premium labels.

13. Roppongi Hills - In Roppongi, this cutting-edge complex mixes dining, shopping, and entertainment. Visitors can check out the Mori Art Museum, gaze out over the entire city from the Tokyo City View observation deck, and eat at hip pubs and restaurants.

14. Tokyo Imperial Palace - The Tokyo Imperial Palace, where the Japanese Emperor resides, is encircled by lovely grounds and old buildings. The palace's grounds are open to visitors on guided excursions so they can take in the architecture and beautiful scenery.

15. Tokyo National Museum - The Tokyo National Museum is the largest and oldest museum in Japan, and it houses a sizable collection of works of Japanese art, antiques, and cultural treasures. Visitors can visit the various display halls and discover the rich history of the nation.

ExploringDifferentNeighborhoods

Japan is a nation renowned for its extensive cultural history, stunning natural surroundings, and distinctive customs. In Japan, every neighborhood has its unique charm and attractions, making it a great place to explore various communities. Here are some Japanese communities you might want to check out:

1. Shibuya, Tokyo: Known for its recognizable Shibuya Crossing, Shibuya is one of Tokyo's liveliest and busiest neighborhoods. Shibuya, a neighborhood known for its focus on youth culture, is home to a variety of shops, bustling nightclubs, and fashionable boutiques. Additionally, you can go

to Yoyogi Park, and Meiji Shrine, and take in the Harajuku street entertainment.

2. Gion, Kyoto: Gion is Kyoto's ancient district and is well-known for its geisha culture and traditional wooden Machiya homes. Take a stroll through Gion's congested streets to see if you can locate any geishas or maikos (apprentice geishas). In this picturesque area, explore Yasaka Shrine, Hanami-koji Street, and take part in customary tea ceremonies.

3. Dotonbori, Osaka: Dotonbori is Osaka's entertainment district and is well-known for its enthralling nightlife and famous neon signage. Take a ride on the Dotonbori River, indulge in delectable street food like takoyaki and okonomiyaki, and enjoy shopping along the pedestrian-only Dotonbori Street. Don't forget to stop by the enormous Crab sign and the iconic Glico Running Man sign.

4. Arashiyama, Kyoto: Arashiyama is a charming area on the outskirts of Kyoto that is well-known for its bamboo forest and natural splendor. Take a trip on a boat down the Hozu River, tour the Sagano Bamboo Forest, and go to the Tenryu-ji Temple. Visit the stunning Arashiyama Monkey Park and the renowned Togetsukyo Bridge as soon as you can.

5. Hakodate, Hokkaido: In the very north of Japan's major islands is Hakodate, a lovely harbor city. Explore the ancient Motomachi neighborhood with its Western-style architecture, climb the picturesque Mount Hakodate for stunning city views, and savor fresh seafood at the Hakodate Morning Market. Don't forget to sample the well-known Hakodate ramen, a regional delicacy.

6. Nara Park, Nara: Known for its roaming deer, Nara Park is a sizable public park in the city of Nara. Visit the park, meet the amiable sika deer there, go to the Todaiji Temple to see the Great Buddha statue, and stroll through the tranquil Isuien

Garden. Visit the Naramachi neighborhood for some shopping and cultural activities as Nara is also recognized for its traditional Japanese crafts and artwork.

7. Sapporo, Hokkaido: The capital of Hokkaido, Sapporo, offers a distinctive fusion of urban attractions and scenic beauty. Visit Odori Park, which hosts ice sculptures and bright flower displays during the Sapporo Snow Festival. Discover Susukino's historic area, which is renowned for its exciting nightlife and mouthwatering seafood. Don't pass up the chance to sample the renowned miso ramen from Sapporo.

8. Asakusa, Tokyo: Asakusa is a historic district in the center of Tokyo and is the location of the famous Senso-ji Temple. Enjoy the local cuisine and shop for trinkets as you stroll down Nakamise Shopping Street, which leads to the shrine. For sweeping views of the neighborhood, head to the Asakusa Culture Tourist Information Center. You

may also see Tokyo's skyline by taking a boat trip along the Sumida River.

9. Hiroshima Peace Memorial Park, Hiroshima: Anyone with an interest in both history and peace should visit this place. The park honors the victims of the Hiroshima atomic bombing and spreads a message of peace. Visit the renowned Atomic Bomb Dome, explore the Hiroshima Peace Memorial Museum, and pause for some quiet contemplation in the park's exquisitely planted surrounds.

10. Hakone, Kanagawa: Hakone is a well-liked weekend getaway from Tokyo and is well-known for its hot springs and breathtaking Mount Fuji views. Explore the Hakone Open-Air Museum for a distinctive outdoor art experience, take a soothing swim in one of the area's many hot spring baths, and travel the Hakone Ropeway for panoramic views of the surroundings. Don't forget to take a Lake Ashi cruise and, if the weather allows, see Mount Fuji.

These are only a few of the many interesting neighborhoods in Japan. The distinct combination of sights, history, and culture found in each area makes it an intriguing and educational destination for tourists. Japan has something to offer everyone, whether they are interested in shopping, history, nature, or food.

Where to Stay in Tokyo

Tokyo provides a variety of lodging options, from high-end hotels to inexpensive hostels. When choosing a place to stay in Tokyo, keep the following popular districts in mind:

1. Shinjuku: For first-time tourists, this vibrant neighborhood is a terrific choice. It is renowned for its exciting entertainment, shopping, and nightlife. Shinjuku also has a large selection of hotels that may accommodate different budgets.

Shibuya, a bustling neighborhood, is well known for its iconic crossing and chic shopping avenues.

Younger tourists who want to experience Tokyo's thriving youth scene frequently visit this location.

3. Ginza: Ginza is the place to go if you want to indulge in upscale dining and lodging. There are upscale shops, renowned restaurants, and luxury hotels here.

4. Asakusa: Asakusa is a terrific option if you want to experience traditional Tokyo. The renowned Senso-ji Temple is located in this ancient neighborhood, which also has a variety of ryokans (traditional Japanese inns) and affordable lodging options.

5. Roppongi: Popular among tourists seeking a bustling atmosphere, Roppongi is known for its exciting nightlife and entertainment. It offers a variety of high-end hotels, cool bars, and diverse dining options.

6. Ueno: The culturally diverse neighborhood of Ueno is home to several museums, a zoo, and Ueno Park. There are a variety of low-cost and mid-range hotels in this neighborhood.

7. Odaiba: Situated on a man-made island in Tokyo Bay, Odaiba offers breathtaking views of the water as well as a wide range of entertainment opportunities. It is home to theme parks, opulent hotels, and modern shopping centers.

8. Ikebukuro: This thriving business and entertainment sector is located in Ikebukuro. It provides a variety of alternatives for dining, shopping, and entertainment. The location is easily accessible by public transportation, giving it an ideal starting point for exploring the city.

9. Akihabara: Akihabara is the place to go if you ike anime, comics, and electronics. This area, which is regarded as the hub of Japanese popular culture, has

a wide selection of themed eateries, electronics shops, and inexpensive lodging.

10. Marunouchi: A business zone with upmarket lodging and shopping options, Marunouchi is situated in the center of Tokyo. For those looking for quick access to transportation, it is also conveniently situated close to Tokyo Station.

You may discover a variety of lodging options in Tokyo to fit your tastes and budget, no matter where you decide to stay.

Dining and Nightlife in Tokyo

Tokyo has a diverse range of food and nightlife alternatives to suit every taste. You can choose from cuisines that are both traditional Japanese food and dishes from around the world. Here are some well-known locations to visit in Tokyo:

1. Shibuya: This thriving neighborhood is renowned for its chic eateries and exciting nightlife. Everything is available, from inexpensive izakayas (Japanese pubs) to upscale sushi restaurants and international cuisine. Explore the area's exciting bars and clubs after dinner.

2. Shinjuku: Home to a large selection of eateries and bars, Shinjuku is another well-liked district for dining and nightlife. For a truly local experience, visit the Golden Gai, a narrow lane filled with teeny pubs and cafes. Rooftop bars are another option for enjoying the metropolitan skyline.

3. Ginza: Besides being the affluent retail center of Tokyo, Ginza is also the location of a lot of upscale eateries. Fine dining options are available here, including sushi omakase (chef's choice) counters and restaurants with Michelin stars.

4. Roppongi: Known for its vibrant nightlife, Roppongi features a variety of posh clubs, bars, and

live music venues. Additionally, you can discover restaurants serving food from across the globe, including American, French, and Italian cuisine. The Roppongi Hills complex, which is home to several hip clubs and eateries, should not be missed.

5. Asakusa: This storied district is renowned for its authentic ambiance and street cuisine. Try some regional specialties including sushi, yakitori, and tempura. Take a stroll along Nakamise Shopping Street after dinner or stop by an authentic izakaya for a sense of bygone Tokyo.

6. Tsukiji Fish Market: For lovers of seafood, a trip to this renowned fish market is a must. To catch the renowned tuna auction, start your day early. Afterward, go to one of the many sushi restaurants for a tasty and fresh dinner.

7. Omoide Yokocho: This tiny alleyway, which is close to Shinjuku Station, is lined with yakitori stands and small, cozy bars. It's a fun spot to try

grilled skewers, drink sake or whisky, and take in the bustling ambiance.

8. Tokyo Skytree: Visit one of the eateries in Tokyo Skytree for breathtaking city views while dining. You can eat while admiring the amazing view, whether it's modern Japanese food or other cuisines from around the world.

9. Izakayas: Scattered around Tokyo, these traditional Japanese pubs provide a relaxed dining experience with a variety of small foods and drinks. While unwinding, you can sample several kinds of sake, shochu, and beer.

10. Robot Restaurant: In Shinjuku, the Robot Restaurant offers a distinctive and interesting dining experience. This outlandish location offers a performance complete with actors, robots, and neon lights, along with a bento box lunch.

Always book appointments in advance, especially at well-known and upscale eateries. Tokyo is a city that never sleeps, so no matter if you're searching for a romantic dinner, a wild night out at the club, or a relaxed meal at an izakaya, you're sure to find something to fit your taste in this dynamic metropolis.

Introduction to Kyoto

The city of Kyoto, which is frequently referred to as Japan's cultural capital, is rich in culture, history, and beauty. Kyoto, located in the center of the nation, is the site of countless ancient temples, breathtaking gardens, and grand old structures. Kyoto provides a fascinating fusion of the old and new, from the famous Fushimi Inari Shrine with its colorful torii gates to the tranquil Arashiyama Bamboo Grove. By participating in traditional tea ceremonies, visiting authentic geisha districts, and indulging in delectable dishes like kaiseki and matcha, tourists may fully immerse themselves in the city's rich cultural legacy. Kyoto is a feast for the senses all year long with its picturesque landscapes, bright autumn foliage, and cherry blossoms in the spring. Kyoto is a place that will make an impression, whether you're looking for peace, inspiration, or a chance to connect with Japan's fascinating past.

Welcome to Kyoto, the historical, cultural, and natural wonder capital of Japan. Kyoto, a city in the center of Japan, is renowned for its myriad old buildings, attractive gardens, and ancient temples. Kyoto skillfully combines the ancient and the new, from the well-known Fushimi Inari Shrine and its stunning torii gates to the serene Arashiyama Bamboo Grove. By taking part in traditional tea ceremonies, touring geisha neighborhoods, and indulging in delectable kaiseki cuisine and matcha, you may get a sense of Japan's rich cultural past. Kyoto offers a sensory experience throughout the year with its stunning scenery, bright autumn foliage, and cherry blossoms in the spring. Kyoto guarantees a remarkable experience, whether you're looking for peace, inspiration, or the chance to immerse yourself in Japan's fascinating past.

Welcome to Kyoto, Japan's cultural mecca where old traditions and cutting-edge city life coexist together. Kyoto, a city in the center of Japan, is famed for its imposing temples, breathtaking gardens, and important historical sites. Kyoto is a city where every turn offers a look into Japan's rich history, from the recognizable vermilion gates of Fushimi Inari Shrine to the tranquil beauty of Kinkaku-ji. Discover the classic wooden Machiya homes in Gion's winding pathways, see geishas glide through the streets, and indulge in the subtle flavors of Kyoto cuisine. Kyoto embodies Japan's ageless beauty with its beautiful natural surroundings, exciting festivals, and zen-like atmosphere. Come and see this enchanting city for yourself, which skillfully combines the ancient with the new.

Must-Visit Temples and Shrines in Kyoto

1. Kinkaku-ji (Golden Pavilion): This famous temple, which is coated in gold leaf, is serenely situated next to a still body of water. One of Kyoto's most popular temples, it provides stunning vistas throughout the year.

2. Fushimi Inari Taisha: One of the most significant Shinto shrines in Japan, Fushimi Inari Taisha is distinguished by its numerous brilliant red torii gates. For sweeping views of Kyoto, visitors can trek through the gates to Mount Inari's peak.

3. Kiyomizu-dera: From its vantage point on a hill, Kiyomizu-dera provides awe-inspiring vistas of the city. It is renowned for its recognizable wooden stage that protrudes from the main hall and offers guests a singular viewpoint.

4. Ginkaku-ji (Silver Pavilion) is famed for its lovely grounds and serene ambiance despite not being clad with silver. The temple is a wonderful location to unwind and take in the wonders of nature.

5. Ryoan-ji: This Zen temple is well-known for its rock garden known as Karesansui (dry landscape). A straightforward yet profound and peaceful area is

created by the 15 strategically positioned boulders surrounded by white sand.

6. Nijo Castle: Nijo Castle is an important historical monument in Kyoto even though it is not a temple or shrine. It has magnificent gardens, wonderful architecture, and renowned nightingale floors that chirp when stepped on.

7. Gion Shrine: A little and endearing Shinto shrine, Gion Shrine is situated in the center of the renowned Gion neighborhood. It is well-known for the geisha culture it is associated with and for its yearly Gion Festival.

8. Sanjusangendo: There are 1,001 statues of the Buddhist goddess Kannon in this temple. Visitors can also stroll through the lovely gardens that surround the temple and take in the spectacular main hall.

9. Yasaka Shrine: Located in Kyoto's Gion neighborhood, Yasaka Shrine is well-known for its vibrant festivals, particularly the Gion Matsuri which takes place in July. The shrine has a colorful ambiance, with bright red gates and lighting.

10. To-ji: The tallest wooden pagoda in Japan, this UNESCO World Heritage Site is renowned for its towering pagoda. To-ji is a fantastic location to see customary Buddhist rituals and activities.

11. Kitano Tenmangu: Kitano Tenmangu, which is dedicated to the Shinto god of learning, is a well-liked destination for students and academics looking for good luck with their studies. When the grounds are covered in vivid pink blossoms during the plum blossom season, the shrine is very beautiful.

12. Rurikoin: This obscure shrine is tucked away in Kyoto's mountains. It is renowned for its gorgeous fall colors and tranquil moss garden. Because

Rurikoin is only accessible to the general public in the spring and fall, it is a genuinely unique and remarkable experience.

13. Kamigamo Shrine: Kamigamo Shrine, one of Kyoto's oldest Shinto temples, is a UNESCO World Heritage Site. It is renowned for its stunning architecture and tranquil forest surrounds, which make it a tranquil getaway from the city.

14. Shimogamo Shrine: Shimogamo Shrine is another UNESCO World Heritage Site that is situated in the Tadasu no Mori forest. It is devoted to the agricultural gods and provides a peaceful haven for guests to explore and take in the surrounding splendor.

15. Daikaku-ji: Formerly Emperor Saga's home, this temple was later transformed into a Hoshuko (a retreat for retired emperors). Visitors can tour the magnificent gardens, and the lovely lake, and take in the tranquil setting.

These temples and shrines provide a window into the rich spiritual and cultural heritage of the

Traditional Gardens and Parks

1. Kiyomizu-dera Temple: Kiyomizu-Dera Temple, which is located on the eastern side of Kyoto, is well-known for its wooden terrace, which provides sweeping views of the city. Traditional Japanese gardens with blossoming cherry blossoms in the spring and bright foliage in the fall may be found on the temple's expansive grounds.

2. Ryoan-ji Zen Garden: Ryoan-ji is a well-known Zen garden in Kyoto and is renowned for its meticulously laid rocks and minimalist style. The garden inside Ryoan-ji Temple offers a tranquil setting for reflection and meditation.

3. Arashiyama Bamboo Grove: This breathtaking natural landmark is situated on the outskirts of Kyoto. A surreal mood is evoked by the tall bamboo stalks, especially when sunlight penetrates the thick

foliage. The grove also connects to the charming Arashiyama Park, which features walkways bordered by cherry blossom trees.

4. Nijo Castle grounds: Known for its majestic grounds and historic structures, Nijo Castle is a UNESCO World Heritage Site. The gardens have beautifully landscaped ponds that reflect the surrounding foliage, serpentine walks, and immaculately tended lawns. The garden of the castle is a prime example of the traditional Japanese idea of "borrowed scenery," in which the design incorporates the natural beauty of the nearby mountains.

5. Gion District: Though not strictly speaking a traditional garden, Kyoto's Gion neighborhood is renowned for its restored streets and ancient machine (wooden mansions). Gion's winding lanes and secret courtyards transport visitors to a traditional Japanese setting and give them a sense of being in another era.

6. Shoren-in Temple Garden: Shoren-in Temple, located in the Higashiyama neighborhood, is renowned for its lovely grounds and serene environment. The garden of the temple has a pond, stone lanterns, and carefully trimmed trees. A walk through the garden exposes secret vantage spots with various views of the surroundings, such as a water pavilion and a stone bridge.

7. Kodai-ji Temple: Kodai-ji Temple is another treasure in the Higashiyama neighborhood and it has several beautiful gardens. The centerpiece of the main garden is a pond with a tiny waterfall that is encircled by colorful plants and stone lanterns. The temple also contains a Zen rock garden, bamboo grove, and moss garden, offering a selection of tranquil environments.

8. Sanzen-in Temple: Sanzen-in Temple is a tranquil getaway from the bustle of the city, situated in the rural Ohara area. The gardens of the temple have

calm ponds, rich vegetation, and paths covered in moss. The Jikido Garden, with its exquisite arrangement of stones, moss, and vegetation, is the highlight and offers the ideal environment for introspection and relaxation.

9. Shugakuin Imperial Villa: Originally constructed as an escape for Emperor GomizunO-O, the Shugakuin Imperial Villa is now accessible to the general public on select days of the year. With its superb landscaping and breathtaking views of Kyoto's mountains, the villa's gardens are well-known. Visitors can explore three different gardens, each with a distinctive layout and attractions including peaceful ponds, luxuriant foliage, and picturesque vistas.

10. Kyoto Imperial Palace Park: The Kyoto Imperial Palace Park is situated around the former residence of the imperial family, the Kyoto Imperial Palace. With its wide lawns, tree-lined pathways, and cherry blossom trees, the park provides a

tranquil haven. The majestic splendor of the palace and its environs can be admired while enjoying a Leisstroll or relaxing on the grassy meadows. The exquisiteness and serenity of Japanese nature and design are on display in these traditional gardens and parks in Kyoto. Visitors can enjoy the tranquil and gorgeous surroundings while immersing themselves in the city's rich history and cultural heritage. Every garden provides a distinctive experience and a chance to connect with Kyoto's natural beauty, from serene Zen gardens to colorful cherry blossoms.

Arashiyama Bamboo Grove

A tranquil and alluring location outside of Kyoto, Japan is the Arashiyama Bamboo Grove. It is well known for its tall bamboo trees, which produce an aesthetically appealing and tranquil ambiance.

Visitors will have a dreamlike experience as they walk through the tall and slender bamboo stalks on their route to the bamboo grove. There is serenity and tranquillity brought about by the rustle of the bamboo leaves and the filtered sunshine that filters through the canopy above.

The swinging bamboo shoots that appear to reach indefinitely toward the sky encircle guests as they move further into the forest. A melodious symphony is produced by the wind rustling through the bamboo, which calms the soul.

Various times of the day offer particularly appealing views of the grove. The pathway is gently illuminated in the morning by a beautiful golden light that passes through the bamboo. As though entering another realm, this gives off a weird and ethereal atmosphere.

The woodland has a lovely and enchanting ambiance around sunset. It was breathtaking to see the bamboo illuminated by the orange tones of the setting sun. A beautiful environment made by the interaction of light and shadow is ideal for taking unforgettable photos.

A distinctive experience can be had by going to the Arashiyama Bamboo Grove at various times of the year. The bamboo grove transforms into a lush and verdant environment in the spring as its vivid green leaves come to life. It's the ideal place for meditation or introspection because of the ambient ambiance created by the soft rustling of the leaves.

The bamboo changes color in the autumn, turning into hues of amber and gold. The bamboo and the autumn foliage combine to produce a striking color contrast. The grove's wonderful ambiance is further enhanced by the carpet of natural beauty made by the falling leaves.

Explore the Arashiyama neighborhood and its neighboring areas for more attractions like the famed Togetsukyo Bridge, romantic boat cruises along the Hozu River, and the ancient Tenryu-ji Temple. These features enhance the overall experience and elevate Arashiyama to the status of a must-see location in Kyoto.

The Arashiyama Bamboo Grove attracts tourists from all over the world, whether they are there to take in the natural beauty, explore the local culture, or just find some peace. It provides a remarkable experience in the heart of Japan with its breathtaking scenery, tranquil noises, and quiet ambiance.

Geisha Culture in Kyoto

The 17th century marks the beginning of Kyoto's long and intriguing geisha tradition. Geisha, often referred to as Geiko in the Kyoto dialect, have been integral to Japan's traditional culture of arts, entertainment, and hospitality.

The historical significance of Kyoto as Japan's imperial capital has been one of the key causes of the growth of the geisha culture there. As the historical and cultural hub of the nation, Kyoto drew a wide range of creatives, thinkers, and entertainers, including geisha, who wished to demonstrate their talents and amuse affluent and powerful customers.

In Kyoto, geisha go through a rigorous training program that often starts in early childhood. Maiko, or young girls, are chosen and brought to an okiya, or geisha house, where they are taught the ancient arts of Japan, including music, dance, tea ceremony, and conversation.

The exquisite and ornate kimonos, complex obi sashes, and unusual haircuts of Kyoto's geisha are recognized as being part of their distinguishing appearance. They follow a historic custom that is thought to accentuate the attractiveness of their lips and mouth by applying white cosmetics to their faces, crimson blush to their cheeks, and blackening their teeth. Geisha culture in Kyoto is a singular and timeless heritage that has been kept and honored for years. The unusual hairdo, known as shimada, is embellished with fine hair accessories. This rich cultural legacy may be traced back to Kyoto's teahouses and entertainment districts during the Edo era (1603–1868) when geisha first appeared as accomplished performers.

The "geiko" and "maiko," or Kyoto geisha, are highly skilled in traditional Japanese skills like music, dance, tea ceremony, and poetry. They spend years of their lives honing these abilities and developing a graceful, sophisticated presence.

The unusual clothing is one of the most recognizable aspects of Kyoto's geisha culture. Geiko and Maiko dress in magnificent kimonos with elaborate motifs and patterns that represent the varying seasons. The ornate hairdos, known as "shimada" and "Wareshinobu," are styled with the aid of specialized combs, hairpins, and wax and frequently adorned with delicate decorations like flowers and kanzashi (traditional hairpins).

Kyoto's geisha culture is closely linked to traditional artistic performances. Geiko and Maiko frequently perform classical music and dance for visitors, demonstrating their proficiency in the drums, the flute, and the three-stringed instrument shamisen.

Where to Stay in Kyoto

The cultural and historical center of Japan, Kyoto, provides guests with a variety of lodging choices. Here are some suggestions for places to stay in Kyoto, ranging from contemporary hotels to traditional ryokans:

1. Gion area: Gion, Kyoto's most well-known geisha area, presents a special chance to experience traditional Japan. Stay here at a ryokan (traditional inn) to fully experience the allure and beauty of the region.

2. Downtown Kyoto: Centered on Shijo Street, downtown Kyoto is a vibrant neighborhood brimming with eateries, shops, and entertainment

venues. For ease and quick access to public transportation, pick a hotel in this region.

3. Arashiyama: This area of Kyoto's western fringes is renowned for its majestic bamboo woods, picturesque river views, and ancient temples. To appreciate the area's natural splendor, stay at a contemporary hotel or a traditional ryokan.

4. Higashiyama District: Kiyomizu-dera and Yasaka Shrine are just two of the renowned temples that can be found in this illustrious district. To be near the main cultural sites of the city, stay in a traditional machiya (wooden townhouse) or a boutique hotel in Higashiyama.

5.Fushimi Inari District: This neighborhood, which is at the foot of the well-known Fushimi Inari Shrine, offers a quieter and more residential ambiance. For an authentic and tranquil Kyoto neighborhood experience, stay in a guesthouse or a traditional Japanese inn nearby.

6. Kyoto Station region: The neighborhood surrounding Kyoto Station is a practical and up-to-date region with a variety of lodging options. For convenient access to dining, shopping, and transportation options, pick a hotel in this region.

7. Kinkaku-ji District: Located in northwest Kyoto, Kinkaku-ji District is a tranquil and attractive neighborhood and is home to the famous Golden Pavilion. To appreciate the splendor of this well-known site, stay in a contemporary hotel with a view of the Golden Pavilion or a traditional Japanese guesthouse.

8. Pontocho District: Located near the Kamogawa River, Pontocho is a small street lined with old-style machiya structures that hold pubs and restaurants. To experience Kyoto's nightlife and eating scene, stay in a ryokan or a boutique hotel nearby.

9. Nijo Castle Area: Situated in the heart of Kyoto, the Nijo Castle Area offers a blend of modern conveniences and traditional sights. Here, stay in a Western-style hotel or a traditional Japanese inn to be close to Nijo Castle and other famous sites like the Kyoto Imperial Palace.

10. Northern Higashiyama: This region is renowned for its stunning temples and gardens, including the Philosopher's Path and the Silver Pavilion (Ginkaku-ji). To experience a tranquil and picturesque setting, stay in a traditional ryokan or a boutique hotel in Northern Higashiyama.

Overall, Kyoto has a range of lodging choices to suit various tastes and budgets. You can find the ideal accommodation to discover Kyoto's cultural and historical attractions, whether you prefer a traditional ryokan, a contemporary hotel, or a guesthouse.

Local Cuisine and Drinks in Kyoto

Local dishes in Kyoto include:

1. Kaiseki Ryori, a multi-course feast that traditionally features the best seasonal foods. Frequently, it includes elegantly prepared foods like sashimi, grilled fish, tempura, and simmered vegetables.

2. Yudofu: Yudofu is tofu boiled in a flavorful broth. It is a straightforward and wholesome dish. With a side of freshly grated ginger and soy sauce for dipping, it is a well-liked vegetarian choice in Kyoto.

3. Obanzai: Using ingredients from the area, traditional Kyoto recipes known as obanzai are prepared at home. It often consists of a variety of small foods like tempura, grilled fish, simmered tofu, and pickled veggies.

4. Okonomiyaki: An savory pancake known as okonomiyaki is created with a variety of ingredients, including cabbage, pork, fish, and mayonnaise. It is frequently provided in Kyoto with a side of regional green onions and pickled ginger.

5. Kyo Tsukemono: Made from regionally grown produce including turnips, cucumbers, and eggplant, kyo tsukemono are pickles in the Kyoto style. They are sometimes used as a condiment or side dish to enhance the flavor and crunch of other cuisines.

Kyoto is known for its top-notch matcha (green tea), which is one of the city's most popular beverages. At a tea house, you can take part in traditional tea ceremonies or savor a cup of matcha. Additionally, matcha is a component of many beverages and pastries.

2. Sake: Kyoto has a long history of producing sake, and the city currently has several breweries in operation. Visitors can take advantage of the available sake tasting excursions to sample several varieties and discover the brewing process.

3. Uji Tea: Uji, a city near Kyoto, is well known for its tea manufacturing. Uji tea is well known for its vivid green color and flavor, especially gyokuro and sencha. To experience the genuine flavor of this regional tea, go to a tea shop in Uji.

4. Yuzucha: Made from the citrus fruit yuzu, which is widely available in Kyoto, yuzucha is a revitalizing beverage. Yuzu juice, sugar, and hot water are combined to make this wonderful concoction, which combines sour and sweet qualities.

5. Kyoto Craft Beer: A number of craft breweries that create a variety of beers are located in Kyoto. Kyoto offers a wide selection of regionally created craft beers, whether you prefer a smooth amber lager or a bitter IPA.

6. Yatsuhashi: Made from sticky rice flour and packed with sweet red bean paste, yatsuhashi is a sort of traditional Japanese confection. It comes in a variety of flavors and variations and is a well-liked snack and souvenir in Kyoto.

7. Mitarashi Dango: This is a kind of rice cake that is skewered and drizzled with sweet soy sauce. In Kyoto, mitarashi dango is a well-liked street meal that's frequently eaten as a dessert or at celebrations.

There are also tasting facilities available at several breweries where you may try their products.

These are only a few samples of the mouthwatering and distinctive native foods and beverages you may find in Kyoto. Kyoto offers a wide variety of dining experiences that highlight the best of Japanese cuisine because of its rich culinary traditions and emphasis on seasonal ingredients.

Last but not least, Kyoto is renowned for its exquisite green tea and traditional tea ceremonies. Visitors can partake in customary tea ceremonies and enjoy the flavor of matcha tea that has just been freshly prepared. The serene and peaceful ambiance of Kyoto's tea shops makes it the ideal place to take in the local culture while indulging in a cup of calming tea.

Introduction to Osaka

Osaka, a bustling Japanese city in the Kansai area, is well-known for its fascinating history, delectable street food, and welcoming citizens. Osaka, the third-largest city in Japan, is a must-visit location for tourists thanks to its distinctive mix of traditional and modern attractions.

Osaka boasts a more than 1,500-year-old, richly illustrious past. It was previously Japan's capital and was crucial to the growth of the nation's culture and economy. There are still traces of Osaka's past visible in the city's numerous historic sites, like the Shitennoji Temple and Osaka Castle.

Consuming the city's famed street food culture is one of the joys of a trip to Osaka. The area is frequently referred to as the "Kitchen of Japan" and is well-known for foods like okonomiyaki (savory pancakes), takoyaki (octopus balls), and sushi. Visitors can experience these mouthwatering culinary delicacies while strolling through the lively streets of Dotonbori and Shinsekai, two renowned food areas.

Osaka is home to a robust entertainment and nightlife culture in addition to its food sector. The city is renowned for its vibrant retail areas like Shinsaibashi and Umeda, which provide a wide variety of goods. Osaka, a bustling Japanese city in the Kansai area, is well-known for its fascinating history, delectable street food, and welcoming citizens. Osaka, the third-largest city in Japan, is a must-visit location for tourists thanks to its distinctive mix of traditional and modern attractions.

Osaka boasts a more than 1,500-year-old, richly illustrious past. It was previously Japan's capital and was crucial to the growth of the nation's culture and economy. There are still traces of Osaka's past visible in the city's numerous historic sites, like the Shitennoji Temple and Osaka Castle.

Consuming the city's famed street food culture is one of the joys of a trip to Osaka. The area is frequently referred to as the "Kitchen of Japan" and is well-known for foods like okonomiyaki (savory pancakes), takoyaki (octopus balls), and sushi. Visitors can experience these mouthwatering culinary delicacies while strolling through the lively streets of Dotonbori and Shinsekai, two renowned food areas.

Osaka is home to a robust entertainment and nightlife culture in addition to its food sector. The city is renowned for its bustling shopping areas including Shinsaibashi and Umeda, which provide a large selection of boutiques, department stores, and specialty stores. The vivacious Namba district, home to neon lights, pubs, clubs, and theaters, is another place where visitors may have a good time at night.

Osaka is home to several museums and art galleries that are worth seeing for visitors looking for a cultural experience. The National Museum of Art exhibits modern Japanese art, while the Osaka Museum of History provides a thorough look into the city's past. Another well-liked destination is the Osaka Aquarium Kaiyukan, which is renowned for its magnificent array of marine life.

The numerous parks and gardens of Osaka are a haven for nature lovers. A lovely place to wander is Osaka Castle Park, which in the spring is covered in stunning cherry blossoms. A serene garden surrounds the Sumiyoshi Taisha Shrine, one of Japan's oldest and most significant shrines, providing a pleasant respite from the busy streets.

Osaka has something to offer everyone, whether they are interested in nightlife, history, gastronomy, or shopping. It is a very welcome location and a fantastic spot to fully immerse oneself in Japanese culture thanks to its lively environment and hospitable residents. many different retailers, including department stores and boutiques. The vivacious Namba district, home to neon lights, pubs, clubs, and theaters, is another place where visitors may have a good time at night.

Osaka is home to several museums and art galleries that are worth seeing for visitors looking for a cultural experience. The National Museum of Art exhibits modern Japanese art, while the Osaka Museum of History provides a thorough look into the city's past. Another well-liked destination is the Osaka Aquarium Kaiyukan, which is renowned for its magnificent array of marine life.

The numerous parks and gardens of Osaka are a haven for nature lovers. A lovely place to wander is Osaka Castle Park, which in the spring is covered in stunning cherry blossoms. A serene garden surrounds the Sumiyoshi Taisha Shrine, one of Japan's oldest and most significant shrines, providing a pleasant respite from the busy streets.

Osaka has something to offer everyone, whether they are interested in nightlife, history, gastronomy, or shopping. It is a very welcome location and a fantastic spot to fully immerse oneself in Japanese culture thanks to its lively environment and hospitable residents.

Highlights of Osaka

1. Naomi Osaka makes history by winning the Australian Open: Naomi Osaka, a Japanese tennis player, is the first Asian to win the Australian Open. She won her fourth Grand Slam championship by defeating Jennifer Brady of the United States in straight sets.

2. Osaka raises awareness of racial injustice: Osaka used her platform all year to raise awareness of racial injustice and police violence. She withdrew from the Western & Southern Open in support of demonstrations over Jacob Blake's shooting.

3. Osaka surpasses Serena Williams to become the highest-paid female athlete of all time, according to Forbes. Osaka received $37.4 million in prize money and endorsement income throughout the previous year.

4. Osaka wins second US Open title: In a nail-biting three-set final, Osaka won her second US Open trophy in September by overcoming Victoria Azarenka. Throughout the competition, she overcame obstacles on and off the court with tenacity and tenacity.

5. Osaka advocates for mental health awareness: Osaka shared her experiences with depression and anxiety, underlining the significance of mental health in the sports industry. She received a lot of support for her bold decision, and it helped to start vital discussions about the difficulties that athletes must deal with.

6. Osaka withdraws from French Open: In a shocking move, Osaka announced her withdrawal from the tournament after being fined and threatened with severe repercussions for skipping required press conferences. She mentioned how important it was to put her mental health and well-being first.

7. Osaka ignites the Olympic cauldron: Osaka received the privilege of lighting the Olympic cauldron at the opening ceremony as the face of the Tokyo Olympics. Her participation served as a metaphor for cooperation, fortitude, and the ability of sport to unite people.

8. Osaka wins bronze at the Tokyo Olympics: Despite being eliminated early in the singles round, Osaka came back to defeat Misaki Doi and take home the bronze in the women's tennis doubles event. She proudly and gracefully represented Japan.

9. Netflix releases a three-part documentary series about Osaka's life and journey: In July, Netflix published a documentary series about Osaka. Fans gained a deeper knowledge of the tennis phenom thanks to the series, which gave them an intimate look at both her personal and professional problems.

10. A new generation is still motivated by Osaka: Osaka has established herself as a role model for numerous young athletes all over the world thanks to her accomplishments, advocacy, and genuineness. She is a great trailblazer in sports and beyond because of her influence that extends far beyond the tennis court.

Osaka Castle

1. Naomi Osaka makes history by winning the Australian Open: Naomi Osaka, a Japanese tennis player, is the first Asian to win the Australian Open. She won her fourth Grand Slam championship by defeating Jennifer Brady of the United States in straight sets.

2. Osaka raises awareness of racial injustice: Osaka used her platform all year to raise awareness of racial injustice and police violence. She withdrew from the Western & Southern Open in support of demonstrations over Jacob Blake's shooting.

3. Osaka surpasses Serena Williams to become the highest-paid female athlete of all time, according to Forbes. Osaka received $37.4 million in prize money and endorsement income throughout the previous year.

4. Osaka wins second US Open title: In a nail-biting three-set final, Osaka won her second US Open trophy in September by overcoming Victoria Azarenka. Throughout the competition, she overcame obstacles on and off the court with tenacity and tenacity.

5. Osaka advocates for mental health awareness: Osaka shared her experiences with depression and anxiety, underlining the significance of mental

health in the sports industry. She received a lot of support for her bold decision, and it helped to start vital discussions about the difficulties that athletes must deal with.

6. Osaka withdraws from French Open: In a shocking move, Osaka announced her withdrawal from the tournament after being fined and threatened with severe repercussions for skipping required press conferences. She mentioned how important it was to put her mental health and well-being first.

7. Osaka ignites the Olympic cauldron: Osaka received the privilege of lighting the Olympic cauldron at the opening ceremony as the face of the Tokyo Olympics. Her participation served as a metaphor for cooperation, fortitude, and the ability of sport to unite people.

8. Osaka wins bronze at the Tokyo Olympics: Despite being eliminated early in the singles round,

Osaka came back to defeat Misaki Doi and take home the bronze in the women's tennis doubles event. She proudly and gracefully represented Japan.

9. Netflix releases a three-part documentary series about Osaka's life and journey: In July, Netflix published a documentary series about Osaka. Fans gained a deeper knowledge of the tennis phenom thanks to the series, which gave them an intimate look at both her personal and professional problems.

10. A new generation is still motivated by Osaka: Osaka has established herself as a role model for numerous young athletes all over the world thanks to her accomplishments, advocacy, and genuineness. She is a great trailblazer in sports and beyond because of her influence that extends far beyond the tennis court.

Tsutenkaku Tower

One of Osaka, Japan's most recognizable sights is the tall observation tower known as Tsutenkaku

Tower. It is a well-liked tourist destination and a representation of Osaka's dynamic culture due to its distinctive design and conspicuous setting.

Tsutenkaku Tower, which rises to a height of 103 meters (338 feet), was first constructed in 1912 and has since undergone a number of modifications and reconstructions. Its current design, finished in 1956, combines modern and conventional architectural aspects.

The Eiffel Tower in Paris, in particular, has impacted the tower's design as does the Northern European architectural style. Its slim form, lattice-like steel construction, and observation deck at the top all show this. Tsutenkaku Tower, however, also features Japanese design elements, such as ornamental lighting, a golden turret at its summit, and a sizable sign that reads "Tsutenkaku."

Visitors can use an elevator inside the tower to get to the observation deck, which is 91 meters (299 ft) above the ground. From there, they may take in expansive views of Osaka and its environs, notably the close-by Shinsekai neighborhood, which is renowned for its vintage vibe and exciting nightlife.

The Billiken Yokocho alley, a narrow alleyway dotted with quaint stores and eateries serving traditional Osaka fare, is one of the tower's other notable features. Visitors can sample regional specialties like kushikatsu (deep-fried skewered pork and vegetables) and takoyaki (octopus balls) here.

The four-faced clock on Tsutenkaku Tower, which chimes every hour and is accompanied by a musical performance including mechanical dolls, is another noteworthy aspect of the tower. This colorful display is a crowd pleaser and has grown to be cherished as a symbol of the tower.

Tsutenkaku Tower is seen as a sign of luck and fortune in addition to its significance in architecture and culture. There is a tiny shrine inside the tower named "Billiken Shrine," which honors the lucky god Billiken. Many people visit the shrine to pray for luck, leave gifts, and make wishes.

Tsutenkaku Tower provides an exceptional fusion of Osaka's history, culture, and breathtaking vistas. Anyone visiting Osaka must pay a visit to Tsutenkaku Tower, whether it's to take in the cityscape, indulge in regional cuisine nearby, or partake in the tower's auspicious customs.

Where to Stay in Osaka

There are many neighborhoods and places in Osaka, Japan, that make excellent choices for lodging. Here are some suggestions for accommodations in Osaka:

1. Umeda: Situated in Osaka's northern region, Umeda is a bustling neighborhood with a wide variety of eateries, shops, and entertainment venues. Having Osaka Station nearby, a significant transit center, makes it simple to explore other areas of the city.

2. Namba: Located in southern Osaka, Namba is well-known for its thriving nightlife, fashionable shopping districts like Shinsaibashi and Dotonbori, and well-known landmarks like Tsutenkaku Tower. The Namba region offers a wide selection of hotels, guesthouses, and hostels.

3. Shinsaibashi: Just east of Namba, Shinsaibashi is a well-known shopping area with a blend of upscale boutiques, cutting-edge clothing stores, and conventional businesses. Additionally, it has good access to public transportation, giving it a practical starting point for exploring Osaka.

4. Nippombashi, sometimes referred to as Den Den Town, is Osaka's Akihabara and Tokyo's Akihabara. Fans of anime, comics, and electronics will find a haven in this area. Numerous shops provide both the most recent technology and collectibles and video games from the past. There are numerous maid cafes and themed eateries in Nippombashi.

5. Shin-Osaka: Staying close to Shin-Osaka Station can be useful if you intend to take day trips to adjacent destinations like Kyoto or Hiroshima. This region is perfect for those who want to travel outside of Osaka because it has convenient access to the Shinkansen (bullet train) and other train lines.

6. Tennoji: This dynamic district in southern Osaka is home to a number of attractions, such as the energetic Tennoji Park, Osaka Zoo, and Tennoji Temple. The region also offers a variety of lodging choices, from high-end hotels to inexpensive guesthouses.

7. Osaka Castle District: Staying close to Osaka Castle can offer history buffs a distinctive experience. A lovely park surrounds the castle, and various hotels close by provide breathtaking views of the famous structure.

8. Kitashinchi: Known for its high-end dining and entertainment options, Kitashinchi is a fantastic option for people looking for opulent lodging and a buzzing nightlife. High-end dining establishments, cocktail bars, and nightclubs can be found in this area.

Overall, Osaka has a variety of lodging choices to meet different needs and budgets. There is a suitable place to stay in Osaka for everyone, whether you like a bustling neighborhood like Namba or a more tranquil one like Shin-Osaka.

Local Cuisine and Street Food in Osaka

The dynamic food scene of Osaka, also referred to as the "Kitchen of Japan," features a blend of traditional Japanese cuisine and foreign influences. When visiting Osaka, be sure to taste these regional dishes and street foods:

1. Takoyaki: The most well-known street dish in Osaka, takoyaki is a round snack made of a batter of

wheat flour and octopus, green onions, and pickled ginger. It is prepared on a hot plate with a special coating of takoyaki sauce, mayonnaise, bonito flakes, and seaweed.

2. Okonomiyaki: This delicious pancake is produced in Osaka with a batter of flour, cabbage, and a variety of toppings like pork, fish, or veggies. It frequently has okonomiyaki sauce, mayo, bonito flakes, and seaweed on top.

3. Kushikatsu: Deep-fried skewers of different items, including beef, seafood, and vegetables, are another specialty of Osaka. The skewers come with a zesty dipping sauce and are lightly battered.

4. Yakitori: Popular in Osaka and great for meat lovers, yakitori is skewered, grilled chicken. Various chicken parts, including the liver, skin, and flesh, can be found cooked over charcoal and basted with a delectable sauce.

5. Takoyaki Senbei: Takoyaki senbei is a crunchy rice cracker snack that combines the flavors of takoyaki. It is a creative take on the traditional takoyaki. It is prepared by baking octopus under a small layer of takoyaki batter, resulting in a crispy and tasty delight.

6. Kitsune Udon: Kitsune Udon is a well-liked noodle dish in Osaka and makes a hearty and satisfying lunch. Thick wheat noodles are used, and they're served in a delicious dashi broth with fried tofu, green onions, and tempura flakes on top.

7. Horumon: Horumon is a classic illustration of Osaka's fondness of offal. A variety of grilled or stir-fried beef and pork offal, including liver, intestines, and stomach, are referred to as horamon. It is frequently cooked to perfection after marinating in a unique marinade.

8. Kushiage: A popular street cuisine in Osaka, kushiage is made of skewered and deep-fried items,

much like kushikatsu. However, the batter used makes a difference. The batter of kushiage is lighter and thinner, which allows the authentic flavors of the ingredients to come through. Meats, seafood, and vegetables are common options.

9. Yaki Imo: Yaki imo, or grilled sweet potato, is a well-liked street food in Osaka, particularly in the wintertime. Over charcoal, the sweet potatoes are slowly roasted until the exterior becomes crispy and the flesh is soft and sweet.

10. Osaka-style sushi, also known as battera sushi, is a distinctive variation of sushi that originates in Osaka. This type of sushi, which omits the use of raw fish, consists of pressed layers of vinegared rice with a variety of toppings, including cooked seafood, tamago (a Japanese omelet), pickled vegetables, and cooked fish.

11. Osaka Sushi: Another regional sushi variant from Osaka, osaka sushi is distinguished by its box

shape and ample contents. In order to make it, sushi rice and a variety of toppings, including seafood, eggs, and vegetables, are placed in a wooden mold and pressed down to form a compact sushi roll.

12. Taiyaki: A favorite dessert in Osaka and all of Japan is taiyaki. It's a pancake in the form of a fish that's stuffed with sweet red bean paste or additional ingredients like custard, chocolate, or matcha. While the filling is still warm and gooey, the batter is baked until it is crispy on the outside.

13. Melonpan: A sweet bun with a crunchy cookie shell that has the appearance and feel of a melon, melonpan is a native of Osaka. Although it is frequently eaten without any fillings, you may also find variants with chocolate chips, matcha, or other ingredients.

14. Kushiage tamago: Skewered and deep-fried quail eggs are the main ingredient in this well-known street food snack. The eggs are covered

in a thin batter and cooked until the outside is crispy but the yolk is left soft and runny.

15. Kakigori: This chilly dessert made of shaved ice is ideal for cooling off in the sweltering summertime. It may also have toppings like condensed milk, mochi, or fresh fruit in addition to bright syrup varieties like strawberry, melon, and matcha.

When visiting Osaka, don't forget to sample these mouthwatering and recognizable local dishes and street food selections. These delicacies will truly introduce you to the city's thriving culinary scene.

Introduction to Hiroshima

Western Japan's Hiroshima is a city renowned for its vibrant culture and extensive history. Perhaps its most notable claim to fame is that it was the first city to be hit by an atomic bomb during World War II. Hiroshima has recovered from this horrible incident to become a vibrant metropolis and a symbol of peace.

The Hiroshima Peace Memorial Park is one of the many historical and cultural sites in Hiroshima. This park honors the lives lost and acts as a somber reminder of the atomic bomb's catastrophic effects. The Hiroshima Peace Memorial, commonly known as the A-Bomb Dome, is a UNESCO World Heritage Site that stands as a potent representation of resiliency and hope.

In addition to its historical significance, Hiroshima has a wide range of attractions and things to do. Local specialties like oysters and okonomiyaki made in the style of Hiroshima are among the city's well-known delicacies. Beautiful natural settings can also be found in Hiroshima, such as the charming Miyajima Island and the lovely Hiroshima Peace Memorial Park.

Hiroshima is a booming modern city with a bustling city center full of retail districts, upscale boutiques, and hip cafes in addition to its cultural and natural attractions. In addition, guests can explore

Hiroshima Peace Memorial Park

A public park called Hiroshima Peace Memorial Park is situated in the Japanese city of Hiroshima. The park spreads the message of peace and the elimination of nuclear weapons while serving as a memorial to the victims of the atomic bombing of Hiroshima during World War II.

The park has a total area of around 122,000 square meters, is located close to the hypocenter of the atomic bomb blast, and has several monuments and memorials strewn about. The Hiroshima Peace Memorial, sometimes referred to as the Atomic Bomb Dome or Genbaku Dome and a UNESCO World Heritage Site, is the focal point of the park and a representation of the city's resiliency.

Other notable memorials in the park include the Children's Peace Monument, which honors the thousands of children who died as a result of the bombing and works to ensure that all children have a future filled with peace; the Peace Bell, which guests can ring in a bid for world peace; and the Cenotaph for the A-bomb Victims, which contains a list of all known victims of the bombing.

Hiroshima Peace Memorial Park also has strolling routes, reflection lakes, and lush vegetation in addition to the memorials. Visitors to the park have the opportunity to learn about the horrific impacts of nuclear weapons and the significance of peace and disarmament. The park serves as a place of remembering, reflection, and education.

The park holds several peace-related events and activities all throughout the year. The yearly Peace Memorial Ceremony, conducted on August 6th, the anniversary of the atomic attack, is one of the most important occasions. People from all around the world assemble for this ceremony to pay tribute to the victims and affirm their commitment to world peace.

The Hiroshima Peace Memorial Museum is housed inside the grounds of the Hiroshima Peace Memorial Park and is open to visitors. With exhibits showing artifacts, photographs, and the personal accounts of the victims, the museum provides an in-depth and emotive narrative of the explosion and its aftermath. Visitors are encouraged to work toward a peaceful future by learning about the horrors of war and the catastrophic effects of nuclear weapons at the museum.

The Hiroshima Peace Memorial Park serves as a somber reminder of the catastrophe that took place there and the necessity of international efforts to promote peace. Both a tribute to the past and a call to action for a society free from the threat of nuclear weapons are served by it. The park works to ensure that the memory of the atomic bombs is never forgotten and that future generations are motivated to work toward a peaceful world through its monuments, displays, and events.

Hiroshima Castle

In Hiroshima, Japan, there is a stunning and ancient castle called Hiroshima Castle, popularly known as Hiroshima-j. Here is an example of how the castle might appear:

Against Hiroshima city's backdrop, Hiroshima Castle stands towering with majesty. It exudes a sense of majesty and power with its towering stone walls and striking black and white color scheme. The castle is surrounded by a moat and is situated within a large park, which adds to its beautiful appeal.

Six stories high, the main tower of the castle, known as the donjon, is crowned by a beautiful, multi-tiered roof covered in elaborate wooden carvings. The tower's white plaster walls are contrasted with the dark gray tiles covering the roof.

The interior rooms receive natural light through tall windows with elegant latticework.

The Otemon, a large wooden gate, welcomes guests as they approach the castle. Stone walls and watchtowers surround this gate, displaying the castle's fortifications. The gate opens to a large courtyard with tranquil surroundings provided by cherry blossom trees and immaculately kept plants.

As they explore the different displays and rooms inside the castle, guests are taken back in time. The interiors feature tasteful traditional Japanese architecture and furnishings. The rooms are divided by sliding paper doors, have intricate screens with exquisite artwork adorning them, and have tatami mats covering the ground.

The observation deck on the castle's top floor, which provides sweeping views of the city and its surroundings, is one of its highlights. Visitors can view the breathtaking surroundings, including the serene river nearby and the park's lush vegetation, from this point.

Additional structures, like tea houses and ceremonial halls, may be seen all across the castle grounds, showcasing Japan's rich cultural legacy. Traditional tea ceremonies and other cultural activities frequently take place in these buildings.

The castle offers a pleasant and tranquil retreat from the busy city because it is surrounded by lush gardens and lovely ponds. Hiroshima Castle is a must-see location for both locals and tourists because of its unique combination of historical value, architectural beauty, and natural surroundings. Its beauty and history serve as a reminder of the tenacity of the Hiroshima population and their capacity to recover and flourish despite hardship.

Miyajima Island

Itsukushima Island, often referred to as Miyajima Island, is a little island in southwest Japan's

Hiroshima Bay. It is renowned for its breathtaking natural beauty as well as for its historical importance and cultural legacy. The island of Miyajima is described as follows:

Miyajima Island is a beautiful island that enchants visitors with its breathtaking vistas and serene atmosphere. The spectacular Itsukushima Shrine, a UNESCO World Heritage Site and one of Japan's most well-known sights, greets visitors as they approach the island. The shrine is well-known for its impressive vermilion torii gate, which during high tide gives the magnificent illusion of floating on water.

The island itself is surrounded by thick forests of maple, cherry, and pine trees, providing a lively and colorful backdrop all year long. Numerous tourists from all over the world are drawn to the area because of the enchanting ambience that the vivid red maple leaves in the autumn and the delicate cherry blossoms in the spring produce.

Miyajima Island's winding lanes are lined with traditional Japanese homes and stores that sell handcrafted goods and delectable street fare. The island is also home to a few exquisite ryokans, or traditional Japanese inns, where guests may enjoy calm accommodations and traditional Japanese hospitality.

The Daisho-in Temple, a Buddhist temple with a more than a thousand-year history, is one of the island's primary attractions. The temple's multiple halls, pagodas, and gardens are open for exploration by those who ascend the stone steps leading up to it. The New Year's season, when many people visit the temple to pray for luck and prosperity, is when it is most busy.

Miyajima Island has a number of hiking trails that can be taken by nature lovers to reach Mount Misen, the island's highest peak. Awe-inspiring panoramic vistas of the Seto Inland Sea and the nearby islands are the hike's reward. Visitors can also stop by Misen Hondo, a quiet temple at the peak where they can meditate and take in the peace of nature.

The wildlife on Miyajima Island is another feature. Wild deer can be found on the island in large numbers, and they frequently approach people in quest of food. Both locals and visitors adore these amiable animals, who have come to represent the island.

Miyajima Island provides a range of outdoor activities in addition to its natural and cultural features. Visitors can go kayaking in the tranquil seas, take a tour of the island by boat, or even try their hand at

Where to Stay in Hiroshima

Are you considering visiting Hiroshima and unsure of where to stay? There are lodging options in Hiroshima for every price range and taste. Here are a few well-liked choices:

1. Hiroshima Station region: Due to its proximity to Hiroshima Station, this region is a practical alternative for visitors arriving by train. It offers a variety of hotels, from high-end establishments to cheap lodging. There are several options for dining and shopping in the vicinity.

2. Hiroshima Peace Memorial Park location: Booking accommodations in this location will put you close to the city's top sights, including the Atomic Bomb Dome and Peace Memorial Park. These historical sites are easily accessible from hotels and guesthouses.

3. Miyajima Island: Just a short ferry journey from Hiroshima, Miyajima Island is well-known for its picturesque landscape and the recognizable Itsukushima Shrine. A few ryokans (traditional Japanese inns) and guesthouses are located on the island, allowing tourists to stay the night and fully appreciate its serene ambiance.

4. Hiroshima City Center: Hiroshima's city center has a range of lodging choices, including pricey hotels and cozy guesthouses. Staying here gives you quick access to the city's diverse nightlife as well as convenient access to dining, shopping, and entertainment options.

5. Hiroshima Bay Area: Think about staying in the Hiroshima Bay area if you want waterfront vistas and a more laid-back environment. A variety of hotels and resorts are available in this region, many of which have breathtaking ocean views. Additionally, it is renowned for its delectable seafood and water sports.

6. Hiroshima University Area: Staying close to Hiroshima University can be a convenient choice if you're in Hiroshima for academic or research-related reasons. For students and researchers visiting the university campus, there are many hotels and guesthouses in this region.

Take into account your vacation plans and the sights you are most eager to see before making a choice. Additionally, consider your hotel preferences and budget. You may choose the ideal hotel to stay in Hiroshima that satisfies all of your demands and improves your whole vacation experience by conducting careful research and making reservations in advance.

stay the night and fully appreciate its serene ambiance.

Introduction to Mount Fuji

Japan's Honshu island is home to the famous and spectacular Mount Fuji. It is the tallest mountain in Japan, rising to a height of 3,776.24 meters (12,389 ft), and is regarded as one of the most symmetrical and stunning volcanic cones in the entire world. Each year, hundreds of tourists flock to Mount Fuji, which is a UNESCO World Heritage Site, to take in its spectacular beauty and explore the surroundings.

In Japan, Mount Fuji has significant cultural and religious significance. It serves as a representation of the country's identity and has served as a source of inspiration for writers, artists, and poets throughout time. Numerous works of art, poems, and literature have been written on this renowned mountain since it is regarded as sacred. Anyone who sees Mount Fuji is captivated by its magnificent surroundings, which include its snow-capped peak and the lakes and woods that surround it.

Many pathways lead to the summit of Mount Fuji, making it a popular activity for both locals and visitors. The mountain is accessible and a variety of amenities, including mountain huts, are available to serve climbers during the official climbing season, which lasts from July to September. The ascent, however, is difficult and calls for both preparation and physical preparedness.

Mount Fuji has a lot more to offer than only its appeal to climbers. There are boating, fishing, and hiking options at the Fuji Five Lakes, which include Lake Kawaguchi and Lake Yamanaka. They also provide breathtaking views of the mountain. In the Fuji-Hakone-Izu National Park, which includes Mount Fuji and the region around it, you may find a variety of plants and animals as well as hot springs and beautiful hiking trails. Additionally, the area is home to a large number of historical and cultural landmarks, including shrines, temples, and traditional villages.

There are many viewing sites and observation decks from which to see Mount Fuji if you'd like a more laid-back experience. In the Fuji Five Lakes area, the Chureito Pagoda provides a stunning view of Mount Fuji, which is framed by brilliant autumn foliage and cherry blossoms in the spring. The Hakone Ropeway gives aerial vistas as it transports passengers on a magnificent tour across the Hakone highlands, and the Mount Fuji Viewing Platform in

Shizuoka Prefecture offers a panoramic perspective of the peak.

This famous mountain offers an unforgettable experience whether you decide to climb it, explore the area around it, or just admire it from a distance. For lovers of the outdoors, thrill-seekers, and anybody looking for peace among the splendor of Japan, it is a must-visit location because of its striking presence, depth of cultural value, and breathtaking natural setting.

Climbing or Hiking Mount Fuji

A very wonderful adventure that will give you lifelong memories is trekking or climbing Mount Fuji. The tallest mountain in Japan, Mount Fuji, rises to a height of 3,776 meters (12,389 feet), and it provides amazing views of the surroundings.

To successfully plan and complete a climb or hike up Mount Fuji, follow these steps:

1. Pick the right time: Early July to mid-September is normally when Mount Fuji is accessible for climbing. The ideal time to climb is during the designated climbing season when the conditions are generally more favorable and the trails are kept in good condition.

2. Create a plan for your climb. Select the climbing path you want to follow. Yoshida, Subashiri, Gotemba, and Fujinomiya are the four main options. Every path has a unique beginning place and provides various experiences. The Yoshida route is the busiest and provides a variety of amenities along the way; the other routes are less traveled but may present greater difficulties.

3. Get physically ready: A moderate degree of fitness is required to climb Mount Fuji. A few months before your climb, begin a training program that emphasizes cardio activities and endurance training. You'll be better able to handle the altitude and the long hikes if you do this.

4. Assemble the appropriate equipment: Be sure to have sturdy hiking boots, layers of clothes, waterproof clothing, a headlamp, trekking poles, a backpack, sunscreen, a hat, gloves, and lots of water and snacks. Additionally, you must have cash because there are stores and shelters where you can buy food and beverages along the climbing routes.

5. Adjust to the altitude: Spend a day or two at the fifth station (the starting point) of your selected route to adjust to the altitude before beginning your climb, if at all possible. Altitude sickness will be less likely as a result.

6. Get going early: To reach the top by daybreak, it is advised to begin your ascent in the late afternoon or early evening. You can dodge the midday sun and enjoy beautiful morning views from the summit thanks to this.

7. Keep your energy levels in check: Climb slowly to enjoy the experience and prevent exhaustion. Regularly rest, drink water, and pay attention to your body. Pay heed to any symptoms, such as headaches, dizziness, or nausea, as altitude sickness can be risky.

8. Achieve the summit, then descend.Be cautious and take rests as you descend to avoid putting stress on your knees and joints. If you come upon loose rocks or slick walkways, be extremely cautious.

9. Think about sleeping in a mountain hut: There are several mountain huts along the routes where you may stay if you wish to break up your trip and rest overnight. But it's a good idea to reserve these shelters in advance.

10. Respect the environment and observe rules: Because Mount Fuji is a sacred mountain, it's crucial to observe rules and respect local customs. Be aware of your surroundings, properly dispose of

your rubbish, and heed any warnings or directions issued by the authorities.

Remember that trekking or climbing Mount Fuji is a difficult task, so it's crucial to be both physically and mentally prepared. Take the essential safety precautions, savor the stunning scenery, and make priceless memories as you ascend Mount Fuji.

Fuji Five Lake

At the northern base of Japan's Mount Fuji sits the picturesque landscape known as the Fuji Five Lakes area. There are five lakes in the area: Lake Kawaguchi, Lake Yamanaka, Lake Sai, Lake Shoji, and Lake Motosu. Each of these lakes provides breathtaking views of the famous mountain.

The most populated and conveniently located lake in the region is Lake Kawaguchi. Particularly at sunrise and dusk, it is renowned for its beautiful views of Mount Fuji. Visitors can take lake cruises, stroll along the lakefront promenade, or unwind in the hot springs.

The largest and tallest of the Fuji Five Lakes is Lake Yamanaka. Compared to Lake Kawaguchi, it provides a more serene and less populated environment. Fishing, canoeing, and paddleboarding are just a few of the water sports available to visitors. Around the lake, there are several campgrounds and hiking trails.

The smallest and highest-altitude lake is Lake Sai, which is also the smallest of the five lakes. Due to its immaculate surroundings and expansive views of Mount Fuji, it is a well-liked location for photographers and nature enthusiasts. The lake is particularly well-known for its spring cherry blossoms and fall foliage, which are both spectacular.

The least populated and most compact of the Fuji Five Lakes is Lake Shoji. It is a hidden gem that provides a tranquil haven from the throngs. To explore the lake, go fishing, or simply unwind on the lakeside beaches, visitors can rent boats or kayaks.

Lake Motosu Is the deepest lake of the Fuji five lakes boasting a maximum depth of about 122 meters.The lake water is so transparent you can see an upside.It is renowned for having waters that are so clear they reflect Mount Fuji's splendor. The lakefront offers opportunities for picnicking, swimming, and fishing.

The Fuji Five Lakes region offers a variety of attractions and activities in addition to the lakes. The .exhilarating roller coasters Fujiyama and Dodonpa can be found at the Fuji-Q Highland theme park, which is close to Lake Kawaguchi. Another well-liked tourist destination is the Oshino Hakkai hamlet, which is renowned for its traditional thatched-roof homes, clean spring water ponds, and Mount Fuji views.

For hikers and nature enthusiasts, the area is a delight. Around the five lakes and Mount Fuji, several hiking trails range from short strolls to strenuous climbs. The Fujikyu Forest Adventure, a well-known treetop adventure park featuring heart-pounding sports including zip-lining and obstacle courses, is situated close to Lake Yamanaka.

The Fuji Five Lakes region provides a variety of lodging choices, including hotels, ryokans (traditional Japanese inns), guesthouses, and campgrounds. Numerous lodging options provide guests with hot spring facilities and breathtaking views of Mount Fuji.

The Fuji Five Lakes region is a must-see location for nature lovers, outdoor enthusiasts, and anyone looking for a tranquil vacation amidst Mount Fuji's magnificence. It provides guests of all ages with an unforgettable and immersive experience thanks to its picturesque lakes, outdoor pursuits, cultural attractions, and spectacular views.

Where to Stay near Mount Fuji

1. Fuji Kawaguchiko Onsen Konanso: From its hot spring baths, this traditional Japanese inn offers breathtaking views of Mount Fuji. Tatami-floored, large rooms and a sumptuous Japanese breakfast are also included.

2. Hoshinoya Fuji: This opulent resort is tucked away in woodland and provides glamping-style lodging with sweeping views of Mount Fuji. The facility offers kayaking, stargazing, a sumptuous kaiseki-style dinner, and other enjoyable activities.

3. Fuji Lake Hotel: Located directly on Lake Kawaguchi's shoreline, this inn offers both Japanese and Western-style accommodations, some of which include Mount Fuji views. Visitors can unwind in the hot springs spas at the hotel or partake in a BBQ by the lake.

4. Hotel Mifuji: This hotel, which is close to the well-liked Lake Yamanakako, offers cozy accommodations and breathtaking views of Mount Fuji. Additionally, visitors can use the onsen at the hotel and dine at the on-site restaurant.

5. Fuji View Hotel: Located close to Lake Kawaguchi, this hotel offers roomy accommodations with Mount Fuji views. Along with several amenities, the hotel offers hot spring spas, a pool, and many dining options.

6. Mizuno Hotel: Located in the center of Fujiyoshida City, this contemporary hotel offers cozy rooms with views of Mount Fuji. A hot spring spa, a fitness facility, and a restaurant serving both Japanese and Western cuisine are among the attractions available to visitors.

7. Fuji Green Motel: Located in the community of Fujikawaguchiko, this inexpensive motel offers easy access to several Mount Fuji area attractions.

Comfortable lodgings, a free breakfast, and a soothing soak in the hotel's hot spring pools are available to guests.

8. Highland Resort Hotel & Spa: This hotel has contemporary accommodations and breathtaking views of Mount Fuji and is close to the amusement park Fuji-Q Highland. Visitors can unwind in the hotel's hot springs, eat at one of its restaurants, or see the neighboring sights.

9. Kawaguchiko Hotel: Located next to Lake Kawaguchi, this traditional ryokan-style hotel provides a window into Japanese culture. Visitors can enjoy traditional kaiseki food, repose in the hotel's hot spring pools, and rest in comfy tatami rooms.

10. Hotel Asafuji: Situated in the Fujiyoshida City region, this quaint hotel offers easy access to both Mount Fuji and the amusement park Fuji-Q Highland. The hotel's restaurant serves a great

breakfast buffet and offers comfortable accommodations, a soothing onsen, and other amenities

Japanese Culture and Traditions

Japanese culture has developed over thousands of years into a lively and complex tapestry. It is a distinctive fusion of historical customs and contemporary influences. The following are some significant facets of Japanese culture and customs:

1. Shintoism and Buddhism: Buddhism was brought to Japan from India, whereas Shintoism is a native religion of that country. The majority of Japanese people combine these two faiths, with Buddhism emphasizing meditation and enlightenment and Shintoism being more focused on rituals and nature worship.

2. Tea Ceremony: The "sado" or "Chado," or Japanese tea ceremony, is a highly ritualized

method of making and serving green tea. It is distinguished by its focus on peace, harmony, and mindfulness. In traditional Japanese tea shops, the tea ceremony is frequently performed and is regarded as an artistic form.

3. Ikebana: Another significant component of Japanese culture is ikebana, the art of flower arranging. It entails picking and arranging flowers, branches, and, leaves with care to perfectly portray the essence of nature. Ikebana is sometimes taught by masters who have devoted their life to refining the craft because it is thought of as a spiritual discipline.

4. Sakura Viewing: In Japan, the appearance of cherry blossoms, or "sakura," is a much-anticipated event. It stands for the grace and fleeting nature of existence. Millions of people enjoy hanami (flower watching) and picnics in parks and gardens while cherry blossoms are in bloom. It is a season of joy and introspection.

5. Kimono: The kimono, traditional Japanese clothing, is a representation of Japanese culture. It usually has elaborate patterns and decorations and is made of silk. Kimonos are traditionally used for formal events including weddings, tea ceremonies, and festivals. They are highly prized for their beauty and craftsmanship.

6. Samurai and Bushido: Samurai were fierce warriors who upheld the stringent Bushido code of conduct. This code placed a strong emphasis on discipline, loyalty, and honor. Samurai played a significant part in forming Japan's history and culture, and their customs are still held in high regard today.

7. Onsen: The Japanese word for hot springs is onsen, and taking a bath in one is a common hobby. Numerous naturally occurring hot springs in Japan are well-known for their purported therapeutic benefits. Onsen etiquette calls for washing before

getting in the bath, showing consideration for other people, and not dressing up.

8. Matsuri: Traditional Japanese festivals, or matsuri, are a significant component of Japanese culture. They take place all through the year to commemorate deities, celebrate the passing of the seasons, and foster a sense of community. Parades, music, dancing, food booths, and fireworks are frequently featured at Matsuri. The Asakusa Samba Carnival, the Aomori Nebuta Matsuri, and the Kyoto Gion Matsuri are a few well-known festivals.

9. Zen Buddhism The Japanese culture has been greatly influenced by Zen Buddhism. It places a strong emphasis on meditation and pursuing enlightenment directly. Zen temples offer serene settings for meditation and introspection, including Kyoto's well-known Ryoan-ji.

10. Calligraphy: Also referred to as "shadow," calligraphy is the practice of writing characters with

an inkbrush. It is seen as a method of self-expression and meditation. In Japan, calligraphy is taught from an early age and is valued for its beauty and accuracy.

The many elements of Japanese culture and traditions are illustrated by these few instances. Japan's distinctive and alluring cultural legacy is influenced by its rich history, art, cuisine, and social norms.

Tea Ceremony

The preparation, serving, and drinking of green tea are the main components of the Tea Ceremony, a long-standing Japanese custom. It stands for peace, harmony, and respect. Depending on the particular school or tradition being observed, the ceremony follows a specific set of motions and gestures. A condensed version of the Tea Ceremony is provided below:

1. Setting up the tea room or other location where the ceremony will take place. This entails setting

out the tea accessories, such as the bowls, scoop, whisk, and container.

2. Introduction: The host and visitors bow to one another as they approach the tea room. The ceremony's topic or setting is then explained by the host.

3. Cleaning: The host washes the tea utensils in hot water to clean them. This action is symbolic of purging the mind and spirit as well as being practical for cleaning.

4. Making the tea: The host uses a tea scoop to measure the tea leaves into the tea bowl. After adding hot water, the tea is quickly whisked with a tea whisk to get a frothy texture.

5. Serving the tea: After the first visitor has taken a sip, the host hands the tea dish back to them.
6. Passing the tea: The host serves tea again, one by one, to each visitor. The tea bowl is given to each

visitor, who then takes a sip while expressing appreciation before passing it on to the following person.

7. Enjoying the tea: After everyone has received and passed the tea, everyone takes a minute to enjoy the aroma, flavor, and presentation of the beverage. It's time to relax, think, and savor the present.

8. Expressing gratitude to the host: After finishing their tea, the guests thank the host for their hospitality and for leading the ritual. Typically, a bow or a few polite words are used to do this.

9. The ceremony is concluded by the host gathering the tea accessories and carrying out a last rite. This could entail cleaning and organizing the serving pieces as well as organizing the tea room.

10. Goodbye: The host and guests bid each other farewell and express gratitude for the event. They

feel rejuvenated, peaceful, and appreciative as they leave the tea room.

It's crucial to remember that the Tea Ceremony is a meticulous and subtle ritual that requires years of practice to master. This condensed form is meant to give a broad overview of the procedure, but each school or tradition may have its own differences in the precise hand movements, objects, and steps. Traditional Japanese sweets or tiny nibbles are frequently served alongside the Tea Ceremony and can be enjoyed before or after the tea.

The Tea Ceremony is not just about making and serving tea; it's also about establishing a calm, spiritual atmosphere where visitors may interact and see the beauty in simplicity. It is a contemplative and attentive practice that promotes peace, gratitude, and mindfulness.

Kimono Experience

Learn about the kimono's history and cultural significance throughout the kimono experience.

- Put on a conventional kimono and have it styled by a stylist.
- Wear the kimono while taking part in a tea ceremony.
- Develop proper obi (kimono belt) tying technique.
- To remember the event, have professional photos made while wearing the kimono.
- Gain knowledge of the various kimono types and the appropriate times to wear each one.
- Experiment with different accessories, such as geta (wooden clogs) and conventional hair ornaments.
- Gain knowledge of the complex craft of kimono fabric design and dying procedures.
- Attend a kimono fashion presentation to witness how the vintage attire is adapted for contemporary looks.
- Buy a kimono or comparable accessories from a store that sells authentic Japanese goods.

- Recognize the rules and protocol for donning a kimono in various contexts.

- Put on the kimono and eat a traditional Japanese meal to completely experience the culture.

- Attend a kimono workshop to discover how to construct one yourself.

- View gorgeous displays of both vintage and modern kimonos at a kimono museum.

- To prolong the life of a kimono, learn how to maintain it properly.

- Examine the many kimono motifs and designs, as well as their metaphorical connotations.

- Attend a kimono dressing lesson to learn the proper techniques for donning the kimono layers and tying the obi.

- Participate in an arts and crafts course with a kimono theme, such as designing your own fabric or making kimono accessories.

To discover how contemporary designers incorporate kimono motifs into their creations, check out a kimono fashion event or exhibition.

- Tour ancient Japanese textile mills to observe how kimono textiles are created and discover the skill that goes into them.

- Gain knowledge of the various regional kimono types and variations, such as the geisha kimono and the summer yukata.

- Investigate the cultural significance of several kimono accessories, including the obi, tabi socks, and geta sandals.

- Attend a Japanese wedding ceremony when the bride and husband are dressed in kimonos.

- Learn how to choose a kimono depending on size, occasion, and personal taste by visiting a kimono store.

- Have a kimono fitting session where a stylist may assist you in selecting and fitting a kimono that fits your tastes and body type.

- Participate in a traditional kimono parade or festival to see how beautiful and cohesive the attire is while wearing a kimono with others.

- see the origins of the kimono as a means of artistic expression and self-representation, and see how modern artists are reinterpreting and recreating the kimono.

- Learn how to interpret the symbolism and significance of the many kimono colors and patterns by looking into their symbolism.

Sumo Wrestling

Japanese tradition has had sumo wrestling as a national pastime for thousands of years. It entails two big, strong wrestlers attempting to push each other out of a circle-shaped ring or touch the ground with anything other than their feet. To retain their size and strength, sumo wrestlers, also known as "rikishi," adhere to a rigid training schedule.

Sumo wrestling has basic rules. At the center of the ring, the wrestlers face off to begin the match. Until one of them is either forced out of the ring or makes contact with the ground with a body part other than their soles, they must establish contact with each other and keep it up. The victor is the first wrestler to win two of the three rounds.

The "heya," or sumo stables, where sumo wrestlers live, train, and eat together, are well-known. The "oyakata," or former sumo wrestlers, who operate these stables are in charge of the rikishi's instruction and growth. Wrestlers get up early to begin their training, which consists of challenging workouts, weights, and sumo-specific maneuvers.

Each stable has its hierarchy, with the more experienced wrestlers, known as "sekitori," serving as a mentor and leader for the less experienced wrestlers, known as "deshi." In addition to helping the more experienced wrestlers in their training, the deshi is in charge of carrying out household duties including cooking and cleaning.

Grand tournaments called "basho," which occur six times a year in Japan, are where sumo wrestling matches are frequently held. Each wrestler competes once every day throughout these 15-day competitions. The competitions are closely followed and watched by many people, who cheer on their favorite wrestlers.

The wrestlers are ranked during a basho according to how they did in the prior competition. The most prestigious division referred to as the "Makuuchi," contains the top-ranked wrestlers. All sumo wrestlers aspire to compete in the top division and become regarded as among the sport's elite.

In sumo wrestling, skill and strategy are just as important as raw power. Different maneuvers, or "kimarite," are used by wrestlers to overcome their opponents. "Oshi" (pushing), "Yori" (grappling), and "Uwatenage" (overarm throw) are a few examples of often-used moves. These moves call for a combination of timing, flexibility, and strength.

The rules and regulations for sumo wrestling have changed over time as the sport has developed. Sumo wrestling in modern times is very regulated, with tight rules about weight, dress, and conduct. Professional sumo wrestlers must weigh at least 75 kilograms, and they represent their culture by donning the "mawashi" during competition.

In Japan, sumo wrestling has a deep cultural significance. It is strongly ingrained in Shinto religious beliefs and is seen as a symbol of Japanese tradition. Before each match, holy water is sprinkled on the "dohyo," the ring, which is revered as holy ground. Before every fight, sumo wrestlers observe traditions to respect their opponents and pay homage to the sport's past.

Sumo wrestlers are respected for their dedication and discipline in addition to their physical prowess and skills. They adhere to a rigid lifestyle that includes a prescribed diet, rigorous exercise, and observance of cultural traditions. Because of its dedication, sumo wrestling holds a unique place in Japanese society.

Sumo wrestling is a venerable sport that has been practiced for centuries and continues to enthrall spectators with its unique fusion of athleticism, tradition, and cultural significance. It is a type of art that displays the strength, talent, and history of Japan, making it an exceptional and alluring spectacle.

Kabuki Theater

Japanese theater that incorporates dance, music, and lavish costumes is known as kokuki. It is renowned for its stylized acting and ostentatious makeup and frequently tells historical or mythological tales. Here is a piece of Kabuki theater that was produced at random:

The Warrior's Revenge: A Tale of Revenge

Scene 1 of Act 1: The Battlefield There is a bloody conflict going on between two competing clans - The main character, a teenage warrior named Koji, battles bravely - Lord Takashi, the lord of the other clan, shows up there and dares Koji to a duel. Koji agrees to the challenge, and the two start a fierce sword duel.

Scene 2: The Warrior's Decline Koji is hurt during the fight and loses consciousness. His comrades carry him from the field of combat - Koji awakens in a little hut, wounded and weak. A wise old man comes to visit him and tells him that Lord Takashi cheated in their combat. Koji vows vengeance, vows to pursue justice, and starts preparing for the big fight.

Act 2: Scene 1: The Training Grounds - Koji receives strict instruction from a famed samurai master. The master helps him hone his skills and teach him new ones. Koji works diligently day and night, pushing himself to the maximum on both a physical and mental level.

Scene 2: The Journey for Enlightenment - Koji sets off on a journey to gain inner strength and enlightenment - He stops at revered temples and practices meditation in peaceful settings - As he travels, he faces numerous obstacles and is put to the test of his fortitude.

Scene 1 of Act 3's The Final Confrontation In a tense confrontation, Koji finally faces Lord Takashi. The stage is decorated with intricate set pieces that depict a gloomy and evil castle. Koji resists Lord Takashi's intimidation efforts despite his best efforts. A massive combat with skillful swordplay and acrobatic movements follows.

Scene 2: Victory and Redemption - Koji triumphs by striking Lord Takashi with a devastating blow - Clan members who had lived under Lord Takashi's tyrannical reign are happy because Koji's victory ushers in a new era of peace and fairness. The play concludes with a joyous dance that demonstrates the community's cohesion and strength.

Koji's journey serves as a reminder of the unwavering human spirit and the pursuit of justice.

Epilogue: Koji is hailed as a hero and a symbol of resiliency. He is honored with a grand ceremony, where he is bestowed with a prestigious title.

This piece of Kabuki theater was generated at random and does not represent any particular traditional Kabuki plays.
The Moonlit Geisha is the title.

The Cherry Blossom Festival, Act 1: Scene 1 Kyoto's streets are buzzing with excitement as the annual Cherry Blossom Festival gets underway. A young geisha named Sakura captivates the audience with her elegant dancing, but she is secretly carrying the weight of a forbidden love.

Scene 2: The Forbidden Love - Sakura is in love with Hiroshi, a samurai from a rival clan, but their relationship is illegal because of a long-running family feud - They meet secretly under the moonlight and have snatched moments of passion -

The threat of being caught heightens the tension in their covert relationship.

Scene 1 of Act 2 is titled The Unveiling of Secrets. Sakura's envious rival, fellow geisha Ayame, learns of her secret love affair. In case Sakura doesn't leave Hiroshi, Ayame threatens to reveal their illicit relationship. Sakura must make a difficult decision since she is caught between her love and her allegiance to her sister geisha.

Scene 2: The Struggle of Devotion Sakura confesses her love to Hiroshi and discloses Ayame's extortion Hiroshi approaches Ayame and swears to guard their love. A lovely garden serves as the backdrop for Hiroshi's challenge to Ayame in a verbal duel. Ayame is won over by Hiroshi's sincerity and eloquence as she learns how much Sakura and Hiroshi love one another.

Traditional Crafts

Traditional crafts, which frequently entail hand skills and techniques that have been passed down through generations, are a reflection of a nation's cultural legacy. Here are a few illustrations of regionally specific traditional crafts:

1. Ceramics made in Japan: Japanese pottery is renowned for its exquisite porcelain and stoneware, and it frequently contains traditional patterns like cherry blossoms or landscapes.
- Mexican Talavera: This hand-painted ceramic, whose origins date back to the 16th century, is renowned for its vivid hues and striking floral patterns.

2. Navajo rugs are famous for their intricate textile weaving, which is done on a traditional loom by the Navajo people of the American Southwest. These rugs frequently include organic colors and geometric designs.
- Kente fabric: Handwoven in Ghana, West Africa, Kente cloth is made from vibrant silk or cotton strips. Every color and design has a significant meaning.

3. Woodworking: - Scandinavian woodcarving: This craft involves sophisticated woodwork and is frequently used to make ornaments and other beautiful items out of wood.

- Marquetry: A method of inlaying wood, marquetry entails assembling tiny veneer pieces to form complex patterns.

4. Paper art: Origami is a traditional Japanese paper folding technique that has developed over generations. Without using scissors or glue, it entails constructing complicated sculptures and figures from a single sheet of paper.

Chinese paper cutting is a traditional Chinese activity that entails using a knife or pair of scissors to cut elaborate motifs into paper. A common use for the cutouts is as decorative items or framed artwork.

5. Embroidery: Hungarian folk embroidery is a traditional art form that entails minute hand

stitching to produce elaborate and vibrant patterns on textiles including clothing, tablecloths, and pillowcases.

- Indian embroidery: With many distinct regional styles, India is renowned for its rich needlework traditions. Some well-known Indian embroidery methods are Kantha from West Bengal, Phulkari from Punjab, and Chikankari from Lucknow.

6. Metalwork: Moroccan brass and silverware is a specialty of Moroccan artists who work with the metals to produce elaborate lamps, platters, teapots, and other ornamental items embellished with conventional designs and motifs.

Japanese sword crafting is regarded as one of the greatest examples of traditional metalwork and calls for extraordinary skill and accuracy. To manufacture a sturdy and sharp blade, steel is folded and layered.

7. Basket weaving: Native American tribes all over North America have a long history of creating baskets. Different tribes have their distinctive

designs and make baskets of various sizes and uses out of natural materials like grasses, reeds, and strips of wood.

- African raffia weaving: Stunning and robust baskets are made from raffia palm leaves in several African nations. Complex patterns and motifs are produced by using traditional weaving processes.

8. Leatherworking: Moroccan leather products: Moroccan craftspeople are expert leather workers who produce high-end leather products like belts, shoes, and bags. The distinctive texture and durability of leather are a result of traditional methods for tanning leather utilizing natural ingredients.

9. Glassblowing: Venetian glass is known across the world for its elaborate designs and vivid hues. In Venice, Italy, artists have been practicing the ancient technique of glassblowing for many years, producing exquisite chandeliers, sculptures, and glassware.

10. Carpentry: The Scandinavian woodworking tradition places a strong emphasis on practical design and natural materials. Examples of these countries include Sweden and Norway. Simple and elegant architectural components, wooden utensils, and furniture are all made using traditional techniques.

11. Lace-making: Belgian lace is well-known for its exquisite bobbin lace and needle lace production processes. Beautiful tablecloths, curtains, and apparel accents are made with delicate and elaborate lace patterns made by skilled artisans utilizing fine threads.

These are only a few illustrations of traditional arts and crafts from many cultures. Each craft is an expression of the creativity and talent of its creators and carries a rich cultural legacy.

Practical Tips for Traveling in Japan

Although many individuals in Japan communicate in English, it never hurts to know a few fundamental words and phrases, such as "hello," "thank you," and "goodbye." This will facilitate dialogue and demonstrate respect for regional customs.

2. Keep cash on hand: Many smaller stores and restaurants in Japan still prefer cash, even if credit cards are frequently accepted in tourist areas. Always have adequate cash on hand, especially when traveling to remote places.

3. Make use of the public transportation system; Japan has one of the best ones in the world. As they are reliable, efficient, and frequently quicker than driving, use trains, subways, and buses to get around. To ride JR trains at no additional cost, think about purchasing a Japan Rail Pass.

4. Respect local traditions and customs: Japan has a rich cultural legacy, thus it's crucial to uphold and respect them. For instance, take off your shoes before entering a traditional inn or someone's home, and observe proper decorum when entering temples or shrines.

5. Use convenience stores to your advantage: In Japan, quick-stops like 7-Eleven, FamilyMart, and Lawson are travelers greatest friends. They are open nearly always and provide a large selection of reasonably priced food, beverages, and other necessities. If necessary, you can also use them to get cash from ATMs.

6. Be considerate of the quiet places: In Japan, there are designated quiet spaces on trains and buses where using a phone or speaking aloud is considered rude. Follow these guidelines and keep your voice low in public areas.

7. Sample the local cuisine: Since sushi, ramen, tempura, and takoyaki are among the delectable local delicacies, Japan is known for its exquisite cuisine. Don't be hesitant to experiment with new foods and cuisines.

8. Make reservations for lodging in advance because Japan may get busy, especially during the busiest travel times. Find guesthouses, ryokans (classic inns), or business hotels that fit your preferences and budget.

9. Purchase a SIM card or pocket Wi-Fi: Having internet connectivity on your phone will be quite beneficial for locating, interpreting, and researching sites. When you arrive at the airport, take into consideration renting a pocket Wi-Fi gadget or getting a SIM card.

10. Remove your shoes at the door: It is usual in Japan to take off your shoes before entering homes, ryokans, traditional rooms, and some eateries. Find

a distinct spot to put your shoes, and make sure your socks are tidy and appealing.

11. Practice appropriate manners in public areas. Japan is renowned for its neatness and order. Follow the rules, such as queuing politely, and refrain from pollution and excessive noise.

12. Be ready for a choice of restroom options: Western-style toilets and traditional squat toilets are among the restroom options you may find in Japan. Learn how to use squat toilets, and always keep tissues or wet wipes on you because not all public restrooms provide toilet paper.

13. Benefit from the onsen experience: Onsens are traditional Japanese hot springs that are renowned for their healing abilities. Be sure to observe the etiquette when visiting an onsen, which includes fully cleaning your body before stepping into the hot spring and concealing your tattoos if they are not permitted.

14. Be weather-ready: Before your vacation, look up the weather prediction and pack accordingly. Dress accordingly for the temperature and weather conditions as Japan has various seasons.

15. Be aware of cultural practices: Japan has distinctive cultural customs, such as bowing as a greeting and saying "Sumimasen" (pardon me) to draw attention. To make your contact with locals more enjoyable, take the time to educate yourself on and respect certain cultural customs.

Etiquette and Customs

When visiting or dealing with Japanese people, it's crucial to respect and follow these etiquette customs because Japan is known for its rich cultural past and distinctive customs. Here are some important manners and traditions to be mindful of:

1. Greetings: It is usual to bow out of respect when meeting someone for the first time or in a formal

environment. The depth of the bow will vary depending on the circumstance, although a light bow is typically adequate for informal interactions. Although handshakes are more frequently used in professional contexts, it is best to take the Japanese person's example.

2. Taking Off Your Shoes: It is usual in Japan to take off your shoes before entering a person's home, some traditional establishments, and even some modern structures. Wear the slippers you find at the door as you enter. When using the facilities, change into bathroom-specific slippers if there are any.

3. Gift-Giving: As a significant aspect of Japanese culture, gift-giving is frequently done to show appreciation or establish and sustain social ties. It is usual to present gifts with both hands and to refrain from opening them in front of the giver. Repaying with a gift of equal or greater value is also considered polite.

4. Dining Etiquette: There are several Japanese dining etiquette rules to follow, including:

- It is usual to take off your shoes before entering a traditional Japanese restaurant and to leave them in a certain location.
- Sit on the floor or a cushion (zabuton) when seated at a low table with your legs crossed or folded. Try not to extend your legs or point your feet straight toward getting people.
- It is customary to say "Itadakimasu" before beginning to eat and "Gochisousama Deshita" to show appreciation for the meal.
- Chopsticks shouldn't be placed upright in a dish of rice since doing so is thought to be a funeral custom. Instead, set them on the chopstick rest or arrange them across the basin horizontally.
- Slurping noodles, particularly ramen, is accepted and even a show of pleasure. However, refrain from talking aloud while you're eating.
- It is polite to eat everything on your plate because leaving food on your dish could be considered

wasteful. Try to take modest servings if you can't finish everything, or kindly request a reduced serving.

5. Tea Ceremony: The tea ceremony, also known as "Chado," is a customary Japanese ritual that entails making, serving, and consuming matcha tea. When

Public Transportation Tips

1. Prepare ahead of time. Before utilizing public transportation, review the routes and schedules to make sure you are aware of when and where you must be. You can avoid hurrying or needless waiting by doing this.

2. Keep an eye out for safety: Although public transit is mostly secure, it's necessary to be on guard. Keep a watch on your belongings and be mindful of your surroundings, especially in crowded places. Inform the driver or authorities if you feel uneasy or notice something strange.

3. Have the right change or a pass: To prevent holding up the line or delaying the bus or train, be sure you have the right fare or a valid pass. The majority of public transportation systems offer a number of payment methods, including cash, reloadable cards, and smartphone apps.

4. Give up your seat: Be considerate and surrender your seat to someone who needs it more if you are able-bodied and occupy priority seating, which is typically set aside for elderly, disabled, or pregnant people.

5. Be considerate of others' personal space: Crowds often form on public transportation, especially during rush hours. Respect others' privacy and refrain from touching or crowding them. To make seating spaces available, place your baggage on your lap or by your feet.

6. Listen for announcements and stops: To make sure you get off at the right stop, pay attention to announcements and electronic displays. You can ask the driver or other passengers for assistance if you're unsure. Asking and checking twice is preferable to being at the wrong spot.

7. Exercise patience and wait your turn: Crowded conditions might occur on public transit, particularly during peak hours. Wait patiently for your turn before boarding or getting off the bus or train. Don't shove or push anyone off the bus, and wait for them to exit before attempting to board.

8. Be considerate of others by keeping noise levels down. Public transportation is a shared area, so be considerate of others by doing the same. Avoid making disruptive noises, talking on the phone aloud, or playing loud music.

9. Obey laws and regulations: Passengers must abide by the rules and regulations that are specific

to each public transportation system. These might include restrictions on what people can eat, drink, smoke, or engage in. Learn the rules and follow them to make sure everyone has a smooth and enjoyable journey.

10. Be ready for delays or interruptions: Things like traffic, bad weather, or mechanical problems can cause delays or disruptions in public transit. Keep up with any service advisories or changes via official channels or mobile apps, and be ready with other routes or transit options if necessary.

Tipping Culture in Japan

In Japan, tipping is not a common practice and is often not anticipated. However, tipping is becoming increasingly typical in some locations as the country's tourism industry continues to expand. The following elements could result in the emergence of a tipping culture in Japan:

1. Greater exposure to Western culture: As Japan grows more interconnected with the rest of the world, it is exposed to more Western standards and practices, including tipping. As a result of this exposure, tipping customs may gradually come to be accepted and used more frequently.

2. Growing tourism sector: Over the past few years, Japan has seen a major uptick in foreign tourists, many of whom are from nations where tipping is customary. This increase in visitors may bring about and normalize tipping customs in the service sector.

3. Changing attitudes regarding customer service: Japan has long been known for its great customer service, which places a major focus on delivering top-notch service without the expectation of a tip. However, if consumer expectations change, there can be a trend toward tipping as a way to recognize and reward great service.

4. The impact of international hospitality chains: As more foreign hotel and restaurant chains establish themselves in Japan, staff members may come into contact with tipping customs through their encounters with foreign clients. Their expectations may be influenced by this exposure, which could result in the emergence of tipping customs in these institutions.

5. Education and awareness campaigns: Attempts to inform both locals and visitors about tipping customs and their advantages may help Japan develop a tipping culture. This can entail outlining the advantages of tipping for service industry employees or offering recommendations on when and how much to tip.

6. Peer pressure and social influence: As tipping becomes more widespread in some sectors of the economy or geographical areas, there may be social pressure to follow these customs. This can cause customs surrounding tipping to spread gradually.

7. Economic incentives: In some circumstances, establishments may offer discounts or other advantages to patrons who tip. These rewards might persuade clients to tip regularly and help foster the growth of a tipping culture.

It's vital to remember that creating a tipping culture in Japan would be a long process and would run up against social conventions and cultural customs. But it's feasible that tipping will gain popularity in the future due to rising globalization and altered customer expectations.

Shopping and Souvenir Recommendations

1. Local Craft Market: Look for one-of-a-kind handmade items there, such as ceramics, clothing, and artisanal jewelry. Purchase unique goods and support regional craftsmen.

2. Boutique Stores: The boutique shops in the city center are a great place to seek high-end clothing and accessories. You'll discover a carefully picked collection of designer products and cutting-edge clothing.

3. Food Markets: Explore the local food markets to indulge in the gastronomic scene. Purchase plenty of fresh local produce, spices, and snacks to enjoy while traveling or to take home.

4. Visit antique stores to find one-of-a-kind furniture, collectibles, and decor items if you enjoy vintage and retro stuff. You might discover genuine unique gifts and undiscovered treasures.

5. Duty-Free Shops: Before flying home, take advantage of duty-free shopping at the airport. You can find a large variety of tax-free goods, including luxuries, alcohol, cosmetics, and fragrances.

6. Visit regional art galleries to view the creations of up-and-coming and seasoned artists. You might come upon a sculpture or picture that perfectly expresses the spirit of your journey and would make a special souvenir.

7. Local Wine and Spirits: If you appreciate wine and spirits, think about stopping by one of your neighborhood vineyards or distilleries to sample and buy bottles of these products. This enables you to share a taste of the area with friends and family after visiting.

8. Traditional Clothing Shops: Seek out shops that focus on local traditional attire. The local culture is represented by distinctive clothing items such as traditional gowns, headgear, or accessories.

9. Outdoor Markets: Visit outdoor markets where you may buy a range of things, including fresh produce and apparel as well as accessories,

souvenirs, and clothing. Its lively and busy atmosphere captures the way of life in the area.

10. bookshops: If you like to read, look through your neighborhood bookshops to uncover books written by local writers or books that explore the history and culture of the place you're visiting. It's a fantastic method to carry on your exploration after getting home.

11. Regional Specialty Shops: Each area has unique specialties. Shops that sell regional goods like cheese, olive oil, honey, or handcrafted chocolates should be sought out. These tasty mementos make wonderful presents or private delights.

12. Outdoor Equipment Stores: If you love to go on adventures, check out the local outdoor equipment shops. You can buy equipment for hiking, camping, or other outdoor pursuits that you can use while on vacation or bring home for further exploration.

13. Spa and Wellness Stores: Spoil yourself with locally made spa and wellness items like bath salts, essential oils, or natural skincare products. These goods can aid in creating a restorative and soothing environment in your own house.

14. Souvenir stores: Traditional souvenir stores are a great place to pick up postcards, keychains, magnets, and other little trinkets to keep as a memento of your journey. These traditional trinkets are very inexpensive and can make lovely gifts or mementos for friends and family.

15. Local Music Stores: If you enjoy listening to music, check out your neighborhood music store for vinyl albums, CDs, or even vintage instruments. Take in the local music culture and bring back some of your travel sounds.

While shopping, keep in mind to set reasonable time and financial goals and to pay attention to any rules or laws about the export of particular goods.

Enjoy your shopping trip and hold onto the souvenirs you buy to keep as cherished keepsakes of your journey.

Packing List for Japan

- Travel permits and passports
Japanese Yen or foreign credit/debit cards as local money
- A map or guidebook to Japan
- A SIM-enabled smartphone or an overseas roaming plan
- A Type A or Type B power adaptor for Japanese outlets
- Seasonally appropriate lightweight apparel (layers during the winter months)
- Comfy shoes for walking
Rain gear or an umbrella
- If visiting hot springs or beaches, a swimsuit, and towel
- Sunglasses and a hat
- Personal care and toiletry goods
- Medication with a prescription, if necessary

- Sunscreen and bug spray - A small first-aid kit for travel
- Records of travel insurance
- High-quality smartphone or camera for preserving memories
- Electronics charger on the go
- Snacks and beverages for the trip
- A travel pillow, an eye mask, and earplugs for sound sleep on lengthy plane or train rides
- A foldable backpack or a tote bag for day trips or shopping - A portable WiFi device or SIM card for internet access on the road - Travel-sized laundry detergent for washing clothing by hand
- Quick-drying or travel towels - If necessary, an adaptor for bathroom appliances
- An app for a phrasebook or a translator.
- A waterproof bag or cover to keep valuables dry during inclement weather

Traditional Festivals and Events

1. Oktoberfest in Munich, Germany: One of the biggest beer festivals in the world, Oktoberfest draws millions of tourists every year. Beer, food, and traditional Bavarian music are all included.

2. Rio's Carnival is renowned for its colorful parades, spectacular costumes, and samba dance. It is one of the biggest events in the nation and a celebration of Brazilian culture.

3. Holi - India: Holi, also known as the festival of colors, is observed all over India. The advent of spring and the victory of good over evil are symbolized by throwing colorful powders and water at one another.

4. Dia de los Muertos - Mexico: This Day of the Dead festival commemorates departed loved ones and combines indigenous and Catholic customs. Families prepare beautiful altars, embellish graves, and take pleasure in festive fare and music.

5. Lantern Festival - China: Thousands of paper lanterns are released into the sky to commemorate this festival, which signals the conclusion of the Lunar New Year celebrations. It represents letting go of issues and beginning fresh.

6. Diwali - India: One of the most significant holidays in India is Diwali, sometimes referred to as the Festival of Lights. It honors the triumph of good over evil and of light over darkness. People exchange gifts, set off fireworks, light candles and lamps inside their houses, and enjoy celebratory meals.

7. Mardi Gras in New Orleans, USA: Also referred to as Fat Tuesday, Mardi Gras is a carnival event

that takes place there. Before the start of Lent, it is marked by parades, vibrant floats, masquerade balls, and overindulgence in food and fun.

Thailand's Songkran festival, which marks the beginning of the Thai New Year, is well-known for its water fights and splashing. People go outside to playfully drench each other with water guns, buckets, and hoses, symbolizing the rinsing away of the negative of the previous year.

9. La Tomatina - Buol, Spain: Every year, the town of Buol hosts the tomato-throwing event known as La Tomatina. To participate in a giant tomato fight, thousands of people congregate in the streets, turning the area bright crimson and making for an unusual and filthy event.

10. Carnival of Venice, Italy: The magnificent masks and costumes used during the Carnival of Venice are well-known. Participants don elaborate costumes and masks.

Cherry Blossom Viewing

1. Arrange your itinerary: The cherry blossom season in Japan varies by area and often begins in late March or early April. By doing some research on the region's specific dates, you can reserve your lodging in advance.

2. Pick a location: Popular cherry blossom viewing locations in Japan include Tokyo, Kyoto, and Osaka. Every place has a distinct vibe and charms of its own. When deciding where to go to see cherry blossoms, take your preferences for urban life, historical attractions, or natural landscapes into account.

3. Participate in hanami events: Hanami is the Japanese ritual of appreciating the beauty of cherry blossoms. To commemorate the coming of spring, many townspeople enjoy picnics, drink sake, and congregate in parks and gardens. Taking part in a hanami party is a wonderful chance to interact with locals and learn about their culture.

4. Visit well-known cherry blossom viewing locations, such as Ueno Park in Tokyo, Maruyama Park in Kyoto, and Nara Park in Nara. These areas frequently contain a variety of cherry trees, resulting in a varied and beautiful display of pink and white blossoms.

5. Visit off-the-beaten-track sites: even though popular locations draw enormous crowds, there are several hidden treasures where you can experience cherry blossoms in a more tranquil and private atmosphere. A more intimate encounter with the cherry blossoms can be had by going to smaller parks, temples, or rural locations.

6. Take a boat ride: Many cities have rivers or canals that are dotted with cherry trees, including Tokyo and Osaka. You may experience the tranquil ambiance and a new viewpoint on the cherry blossoms by taking a boat ride around these canals.

Attend cherry blossom festivals: Cherry blossom season is a time when many cities and towns commemorate the blooming of the cherry trees with festivals. These celebrations frequently feature food booths, parades, and concerts. To experience the festive mood, check the schedules of nearby festivals and arrange your visit appropriately.

8. Catch the moment: Cherry blossoms produce a beautiful scene that is well-known for photography. Bring your camera so you can record the cherry blossoms' stunning splendor. Don't forget to set aside some time to just unwind, sit back, and take it all in.

9. Snack on delicacies associated with cherry blossoms: During this season, many food and drink items in Japan are flavored with cherry blossoms. A typical treat created with sticky rice and cherry leaves is sakura mochi. You may also try sakura tea. The overall experience of cherry blossoms is enhanced by their distinctive tastes.

10. Be prepared for crowds: Viewing cherry blossoms is a well-liked activity in Japan, and many popular locations can become crowded, particularly on weekends and at peak bloom. To escape the crowds and have a more enjoyable experience, consider going early in the morning or on a weekday. Be prepared for enormous crowds.

11. Respect the cherry blossoms: Cherry blossoms are deeply symbolic and important to Japanese culture. Be mindful of the plants and the environment when visiting cherry blossom locations. Do not climb or shake the trees, and properly dispose of your rubbish.

12. Take pleasure in the night illuminations: several cherry blossom locations provide night illuminations, when the trees are lit up with vibrant lights. If they are offered in the place you've selected, these light shows create a magnificent atmosphere and are worth seeing.

Always remember to check the most recent travel warnings and abide by any rules or limitations that may be in effect while you are there. You can have an unforgettable cherry blossom viewing experience in Japan with the right preparation and awareness.

Summer Festivals (Matsuri)

1. The festival of fireworks, Hanabi Matsuri
Any seaside area with sufficient room for fireworks
- Entertainment: a spectacular fireworks display, food booths, traditional music and dance performances, a ritual to release lanterns, and a fashion show including summer kimonos.

2. The Bon Dance Festival, or Bon Odori Matsuri
- Setting: Outdoor location with a sizable dance floor
- Entertainment includes tea ceremony demonstrations, taiko drum performances, yukata rental and dressing, carnival games, and traditional Japanese folk dance (bon odori).

3. Natsu Matsuri (Summer Festival) - Location: Park or large outdoor space - Activities: Carnival rides and games, live music performances, food stalls serving a variety of street fare, shaved ice desserts, cultural performances like Awa Odori (a traditional dance from Tokushima Prefecture), lantern-making workshops

4. Obon Matsuri - Site: Buddhist or Shinto temple grounds
- Events include a ceremony to light lanterns, customary prayers and rituals, folk music, and dancing, tea ceremonies, calligraphy classes, food stands selling vegetarian fare, and an arts and crafts market.

Tanabata Matsuri (Star Festival) is held in the fifth month of the lunar calendar.- Activities include writing wishes on colorful paper strips and hanging them from bamboo branches, seeing traditional music and dance performances, competing in cosplay, viewing cultural displays and demonstrations, and eating at food stands selling a variety of street fare and traditional treats.

6. Awa Odori Matsuri - Tokushima City, Tokushima Prefecture - Location: Streets - Activities: Awa Odori dance performances by various dance troupes; traditional music performing; taiko drumming; lantern parades; street food vendors providing local specialties; fireworks show

7. Nebuta Matsuri - Aomori City, Aomori Prefecture - Activities: Large illuminated floats (nebula) march through the streets; traditional drums and flutes performing; dance performances; taiko drum competitions; neighborhood food stalls; traditional crafts and art demonstrations; fireworks show.

8. Gion Matsuri - Kyoto City, Kyoto Prefecture - Events: Traditional processions with hooded floats (Kamaboko), participants dressed in period attire,

ceremonial activities at Yasaka Shrine, food stands selling Kyoto cuisine, tea ceremonies, and traditional arts and crafts exhibitions

Autumn Foliage Viewing

Japan is especially lovely in the autumn when the leaves are changing and the countryside is covered in a gorgeous tapestry of reds, oranges, and yellows. The following are some of the top locations in Japan to see the fall foliage:

1. Kyoto: One of the best places to see the fall leaves is Kyoto, which is known for its traditional temples and gardens. Many locations, like Kiyomizu-dera, Tofuku-ji, and Arashiyama, offer breath-taking views of the brilliant autumn hues set against old structures.

2. Nikko: A short drive from Tokyo, Nikko is renowned for its UNESCO World Heritage sites and breathtaking natural scenery. Autumn foliage viewing is very popular at Nikko National Park,

where picturesque areas like Lake Chuzenji and the Kegon Falls provide breathtaking vistas.

3. Mount Fuji: During the fall, Mount Fuji, the famous volcano and national emblem of Japan, is surrounded by stunning autumnal foliage. Hakone and the nearby Fuji Five Lakes both provide breathtaking views of the mountain and the changing leaves.

4. Takayama: This ancient settlement in the Japanese Alps is renowned for its traditional architecture, congested streets, and changing leaves in the fall. Many maple and ginkgo trees turn vivid colours of red and yellow in the autumn, making the Hida Folk Village and the Shibuyama Village attractive places to observe the autumn foliage.

5. Nara: Another fantastic location for autumn foliage, Nara is known for its historic temples and hospitable deer population. The famed Todai-ji Temple is located in Nara Park, which is a

well-liked location to view the autumnal foliage, particularly in the vicinity of the Isui-en Garden and Kasuga Grand Shrine.

6. Hakone: This well-known hot spring resort town boasts spectacular autumn color and is situated in the Fuji-Hakone-Izu National Park. Panorama views of the surrounding mountains and Lake Ashi are available from the Hakone Open-Air Museum and the Hakone Ropeway, with the autumn foliage giving an extra dimension of beauty.

7. Daisetsuzan National Park: Situated on the northernmost island of Japan, Hokkaido, Daisetsuzan National Park is renowned for its untamed wildness and rocky mountains. The park is transformed with vibrant foliage in the fall, making it a well-liked location for trekking and photography.

New Year Celebrations

The New Year is one of the most significant and well-observed holidays in Japan. Here are a few customary and well-liked ways to ring in the new year in Japan:

1. Shigatsu: In Japan, New Year's Day is referred to as Shgatsu. During this time, a lot of Japanese people go to shrines and temples to pray for luck and prosperity in the upcoming year. On New Year's Day, Meiji Shrine in Tokyo attracts a large crowd and is one of the most well-known tourist destinations.

2. Osechi Ryori: In Japan, Osechi Ryori is a customary New Year's feast. It consists of a variety of dishes that have been expertly cooked and artistically placed to bring prosperity and fortune for the New Year. Each meal has a symbolic connotation, such as the long life of shrimp, the health of black beans, or the fecundity of herring roe.

3. Hatsumode: The first trip to a temple or shrine in the New Year is known as Hatsumode. People line up to make their New Year's resolutions and to offer prayers for prosperity, well-being, and happiness. The most well-known locations for Hatsumode include Kyoto's Fushimi Inari Taisha and Tokyo's Senso-ji Temple.

4. Joya no Kane: Joya no Kane is a traditional Buddhist rite in which temple bells are rung 108 times at the stroke of midnight on New Year's Eve to represent the purification of sins and the beginning of the new year with a clean slate. This practice is frequently performed at nearby temples, and it is thought that the sound of the bells ringing throughout the nation will drive away evil spirits and bring good fortune.

5. Toshikoshi Soba: Buckwheat noodles are used in this traditional New Year's Eve dish. The transition from the previous year to the current year is

represented by the long noodles. Toshikoshi Soba is frequently consumed by families before midnight as a means to say goodbye to the previous year and welcome the new one.

6. Countdown Events: In recent years, Japan has embraced the Western practice of countdown events. Numerous cities host massive countdown celebrations that include live music, pyrotechnics, and light displays. At Tokyo's Shibuya Crossing, where tens of thousands of people assemble to ring in the New Year, the country's most well-known countdown celebration takes place.

Outdoor Activities and Nature

1. Hiking: Discover nearby trails, take in the splendor of nature, and get a fantastic workout. Don't forget to pack lots of water and dress comfortably.

2. Go camping and spend the night outside in a tent. Take in the peace of nature while spending time with loved ones around a campfire.

3. Kayaking or canoeing: Paddle your way across tranquil lakes or rivers. Through this pastime, you may commune with nature and take in the tranquility of the river.

4. Spotting wildlife: Take a nature walk while armed with a pair of binoculars to look for birds, deer, or other types of animals. Being able to watch

animals in their natural environment can be quite rewarding.

5. Have a picnic in the park: Pack a picnic basket with some delectable food and head to a park nearby for a leisurely picnic. Get some fresh air and spend the day relaxing in the great outdoors.

6. Fishing: Take a tranquil day to cast your line into the water to catch some fish. Fishing is a terrific way to reconnect with nature and can be both exhilarating and calming.

7. Biking: Ride your bike through beautiful paths or trails. Along with getting some fresh air and exercise, you'll get to take in the splendor of nature.

8. Geocaching: By taking part in geocaching, you can discover hidden treasures. While exploring outdoors, use GPS coordinates to find hidden caches and experience the excitement of the search.

9. Capture the beauty of wildlife by taking pictures of it in its natural habitat. When attempting to get images of birds, squirrels, or other creatures in their natural habitat, patience, and keen observational abilities are essential.

10. Rock climbing: Push your physical and mental limits by scaling cliffs or rock formations. You can experience nature in a new way when participating in this thrilling activity while pushing your physical and mental boundaries.

11. Go on a scavenger hunt in a nearby park or forest to discover items from nature on your list, such as leaves, rocks, or flowers. For people of all ages, this is a fun and instructive pastime.

12. Gardening: Create a garden in your backyard to get in touch with nature. It can be satisfying and relaxing to work in the dirt, sow seeds, and watch your plants develop.

13. Nature meditation or yoga: Locate a serene area in nature and engage in some meditation or yoga. You can unwind and relax by being in such a peaceful environment.

Hiking and Nature Trails

1. Mount Fuji Trail: Possibly the most well-known and recognizable hiking route in Japan, the Mount Fuji Trail gives hikers the opportunity to ascend to the top of the country's tallest peak. Starting at station number five, the trail leads walkers through a variety of topographies, including forests, volcanic ash, and rocky ground. Amazing views may be seen from the summit, especially at sunrise.

2. Kumano Kodo Trail: The Kumano Kodo Trail is a network of historic pilgrimage paths that connects the Kii Peninsula to three significant shrines. Visitors can explore Japan's spiritual and environmental heritage by hiking along these pathways. The trail offers a distinctive cultural and

scenic experience as it winds through forests, mountains, and rural communities.

3. Nakasendo Trail: During the Edo era, a historic road called the Nakasendo Trail linked Kyoto and Tokyo. Currently, the trail allows hikers to experience picturesque post towns, verdant farmland, and peaceful woodlands while getting a look into Japan's historical past. Because the trail is divided into manageable chunks, all levels of walkers can use it.

4. Yakushima Island: Dubbed the "Jurassic Park" of Japan, Yakushima Island has a number of hiking paths that take visitors through centuries-old cedar forests and to breathtaking mountain summits. The well-known Yakusugi trees, some of which are thousands of years old, are also found on the island. Visitors can fully appreciate Japan's natural beauty and feel awe and tranquility while hiking on Yakushima.

5. Tateyama Kurobe Alpine Route: The Tateyama Kurobe Alpine Route traverses the Northern Japan Alps and is a well-known mountain route. With the help of the route's many kinds of transit, including cable cars, buses, and ropeways, hikers can visit various stretches of the trail. Hikers may take in the spectacular alpine scenery along the trip, which includes snow-capped peaks, soaring cliffs, and clear lakes.

6. Shirakami Sanchi: Shirakami Sanchi, a UNESCO World Heritage site in northern Honshu, is home to one of the last primeval beech woods still standing in the world. There are numerous hiking trails in the area that lead visitors through thick forests, alongside clean rivers, and up to panoramic vistas. The trails also give visitors the chance to see many bird species, bears, and Japanese macaques.

Skiing and Snowboarding

1. Gliding down snowy slopes using equipment known as skis or snowboards is a common activity in the winter sports of skiing and snowboarding.

2. To navigate the icy terrain and execute numerous tricks and movements, skiers and snowboarders need balance, coordination, and strength.

3. While snowboarding uses a single wide board coupled with boots, skiing includes the use of two long, narrow skis.

4. While a snowboarder uses their body motions to control the board, a skier uses poles to help with balance and propulsion.

5. From novices to elite athletes, people of all ages and skill levels can enjoy skiing and snowboarding.

6. Ski resorts have beginner, intermediate, and expert-level slopes and trails for skiers and snowboarders to choose from.

7. You can practice skiing and snowboarding on slopes that have been groomed, in parks with jumps and rails, or in the backcountry where the snow is new and untracked.

8. Because skiing and snowboarding include risky activities, players are urged to wear helmets, abide by the mountain's rules, and pay attention to their surroundings.

9. Skiing and snowboarding are competitive sports as well as enjoyable leisure activities. Professional snowboarding and skiing competitions are held all around the world, including at the Winter Olympics.

10. You can experience freedom and heart-pounding thrills while snowboarding or skiing down a

mountain while surrounded by stunning snowy scenery.

11. Skiing and snowboarding are also excellent forms of exercise because they work out the entire body, activate numerous muscle groups, and enhance cardiovascular fitness.

12. For novices, learning to ski or snowboard may require instruction from a certified instructor. Individuals can lower their risk of injury and improve their technique by taking classes.

13. Depending on one's desire and level of dedication to the sport, skis, snowboards, bindings, and boots can be rented or purchased.

14. Over the years, several skiing and snowboarding methods and styles—such as alpine skiing, freestyle skiing, freeride skiing, and snowboard freestyle, to mention a few—have developed.

15. The communities for skiing and snowboarding are active and social, with many aficionados congregating at ski resorts, mountain huts, or online forums to exchange stories, advice, and techniques.

16. Snowboarding and skiing are weather-dependent sports.

Scenic Parks and Gardens

1. Tokyo's Shinjuku Gyoen National Garden This large garden is a tranquil haven in the midst of Tokyo's hectic urban landscape. It has a range of sceneries, such as formal French gardens, English landscapes, and traditional Japanese gardens. The park is particularly well-known for its spring cherry blossoms, which cover the garden in vivid pink hues.

2. Kanazawa's Kenrokuen Garden - Kenrokuen Garden is a literary masterpiece and one of Japan's top three gardens. It has all six qualities that make a superb garden: openness, serenity, artifice,

antiquity, watercourses, and sweeping views. This garden is a wonderful jewel with its immaculately kept grounds, exquisite tea buildings, and picturesque ponds.

3. Kairakuen Garden, Mito – Listed among the top three gardens in Japan, Kairakuen Garden is well-known for its plum blossoms. More than 3,000 plum trees can be found in the garden, and they bloom in the early spring with vivid hues. The pathways are perfect for leisurely strolls, and visitors can sample food and tea with a plum flavor while taking in the tranquil views of the plum groves.

4. Nijo Castle Gardens, Kyoto - Nestled within Nijo Castle's grounds, Kyoto's Nijo Castle Gardens provide a calm respite from the bustle of the city. A pond, water channels, and stone lanterns are just a few of the classic Japanese landscaping features found in the gardens. Wandering through the perfectly kept gardens, guests may take in the

seasonal flowers, vivid greenery, and stunning architecture of the neighboring structures.

5. Ritsurin Garden, Takamatsu - Ritsurin Garden in Takamatsu is one of Japan's most stunning traditional gardens and provides tourists with a magical experience. The garden has breathtaking scenery, including undulating hills, peaceful ponds, and exquisitely trimmed trees and bushes. The garden is covered in a tapestry of reds, oranges, and yellows during the beautiful autumn foliage, which is one of its most celebrated features.

Tokyo's Hama-rikyu Gardens are sixth. Hama-rikyu Gardens, a historic garden with a long history extending back centuries, are located in the heart of Tokyo. The garden offers guests the chance to participate in a traditional tea ceremony in addition to its magnificent landscapes. The garden is a well-liked location for photographers due to its breathtaking vistas of the city skyline.

7. The Gifu village of Shirakawa-go Shirakawa-go Village, a UNESCO World Heritage site and picturesque park famed for its traditional gassho-zukuri homes and picturesque settings, is situated in the isolated mountains of Gifu Prefecture. The community is tucked away in a valley with stunning views of the mountains and rice fields. Visitors can stroll through the town, enjoy the peaceful atmosphere, and even book a room in one of the old thatched-roof homes converted to guesthouses.

8. Ashikaga Flower Park, Tochigi - This magnificent flower park is noted for its wisteria tunnel, which blooms with fragrant cascades of wisteria flowers in spring. Tulips, roses, and hydrangeas are just a few of the more flower displays in the park that provide a spectacular explosion of color all year long. During special events, the park also offers stunningly lit nighttime views, which add to the enchanting mood.

9. Shimane's Adachi Museum of Art and Gardens - The Adachi Museum of Art is renowned for its vast collection of contemporary Japanese art, which is well complemented by its stunning grounds. The gardens' traditional Japanese aesthetics-inspired design is evident in their painstakingly tended grounds, tranquil ponds, and strategically placed rocks and bridges. Visitors can appreciate the natural and artistic beauty, resulting in a peaceful environment.

Hot Springs and Onsen

1. Mount Fuji Onsen: This Japanese onsen, which is situated at the foot of Mount Fuji, provides stunning views of the famous volcano. Visitors can unwind in the soothing hot springs while taking in the magnificent surroundings. The onsen also has a range of indoor and outdoor baths and traditional Japanese-style buildings.

2. Paradise Springs Resort: Located in Colorado's Rocky Mountains, this opulent hot springs resort

provides a serene retreat from the day-to-day commotion. Visitors can relax in a variety of natural hot spring pools, each with its own distinct temperature and mineral makeup, surrounded by lush forests and snow-capped hills.

3. Iceland's Blue Lagoon: The Blue Lagoon, one of the most well-known geothermal spas in the world, is famed for its milky blue waters and therapeutic benefits. As they soak in the warm geothermal pools, visitors can take in the dramatic volcanic scenery. Additionally, the resort has amenities including saunas, steam rooms, and opulent spa services.

4. Gellert Baths: The Gellert Baths are a renowned thermal spa complex with exquisite Art Nouveau architecture that is situated in Budapest, Hungary. Numerous thermal pools with varied temperatures, as well as saunas, steam rooms, and plunge pools, are all included in the baths. Visitors can splurge on

opulent spa services and take pleasure in the serene setting of these historic baths.

5. Pamukkale Thermal Pools: Pamukkale is a natural wonder in southwest Turkey known for its bizarre white terraces of calcium-rich mineral water. Warm thermal pools are available for visitors to soak in, and they are thought to provide therapeutic benefits for several diseases. The website also features archaeological locations and remains from the Roman era.

6. Banff Upper Hot Springs: Situated in Canada's Banff National Park, these hot springs provide breathtaking views of the mountains and the untamed environment in the area. Particularly in the winter, the naturally heated mineral water is calming and unwinding. Additionally, the location has a historic bathhouse and spa services.

7. Beppu Hot Springs: With a wide variety of hot springs to select from, Beppu, Japan, is referred to

as the "Onsen Capital" of the nation. This includes uncommon onsen varieties like mud baths and sand baths. Additionally available to visitors are steam baths, foot baths, and even theme parks with an onsen theme.

8. Ma'in Hot Springs: Ma'in Hot Springs, located in Jordan, is a lonely oasis surrounded by arid desert plains. Natural pools and waterfalls are created as the mineral-rich water from the hot springs rushes down limestone cliffs. Relaxing in the warm water while admiring the spectacular views of the dramatic surrounding is an option for visitors.

9. Chena Hot Springs: Chena Hot Springs is a natural geothermal hot spring resort that is situated in Alaska, United States. In addition to the hot springs, visitors can go dog sledding, ice fishing, or watch the aurora borealis. Additionally, the resort has an unusual rock lake and an Ice Museum with ice sculptures.

10. Kusatsu Onsen: Known for its excellent, sulfur-rich waters, Kusatsu Onsen is one of Japan's most well-known hot spring resorts. Numerous public and private bathhouses, foot baths, and water fountains where visitors can drink mineral-rich water are all included in the onsen. Visitors can also stroll around the old streets and take in the lively ambiance of this hot spring town.

Recommended Itineraries

1. Kyoto and Tokyo (7 to 10 days)

- Begin your journey in Tokyo, where you may visit well-known sites like the Meiji Shrine, Shibuya Crossing, and the Tokyo Skytree.

- Spend the day discovering Asakusa's historical neighborhood, including the neighboring Tokyo National Museum and Senso-ji Temple.

- Travel to Nikko for the day to see the magnificent Toshogu Shrine and take in the breathtaking surroundings.

- Visit Kyoto and its renowned Arashiyama Bamboo Grove and Kinkaku-ji (Golden Pavilion).

- Discover the Kiyomizu-Dera Temple and the Gion geisha area in Higashiyama's historic neighborhood.

- Visit Nara for the day; it is renowned for its historic temples and the amiable deer that walk freely in Nara Park.

- Visit Fushimi Inari Taisha, which is known for its countless torii gates, to cap off your journey.

2. Miyajima, Osaka, and Hiroshima (7-10 days)
- Start your journey in Osaka, where you may see places like the Osaka Aquarium Kaiyukan, Dotonbori Street, and Osaka Castle.
- Visit Hiroshima for the day and take in the Peace Memorial Park and Museum as well as the famous Hiroshima Castle. Take a ferry to the island of Miyajima, which is notable for the Itsukushima Shrine's floating torii gate.
- Spend a day exploring the breathtaking island, taking in the Daisho-in Temple and Mount Misen's 360-degree views.
- Return to Osaka and spend a day dining and shopping in the vibrant Namba neighborhood.
- To find out more about the rich cultural past of the city, visit the Osaka Museum of History.
- Visit Himeji Castle, one of Japan's most well-known and well-preserved castles, on a day trip to the quaint town of Himeji.

- Visit Osaka crowded Kuromon Ichiba Market to cap off your journey.

3. The 7–10-day Hokkaido and Sapporo Snow Festival

- Begin your journey in Sapporo and take in the annual Sapporo Snow Festival, which features breathtaking ice sculptures and winter activities.
- Discover the origins of beer in Japan and try some regional brews by visiting the Sapporo Beer Museum.
- Visit Otaru for the day; it is a picturesque canal town famous for its glassworks and exquisitely preserved old structures.
- Visit the Asahiyama Zoo in Asahikawa, one of the biggest zoos in Japan, which is renowned for its polar bears.
- Discover the Daisetsuzan National Park's breathtakingly beautiful natural surroundings, including the charming Blue Pond and the lovely Furano flower fields (during the summer).

- Visit Hakodate and take the Hakodate Ropeway to the summit of Mount Hakodate for stunning city views.
- Indulge in delectable seafood at the Hakodate Morning Market and explore Motomachi's ancient area.
- Visit the renowned Noboribetsu Onsen, renowned for its hot springs and volcanic activity, to cap off your journey.

4. Visit Ishigaki Island and Okinawa (7 days)
- Start your journey in Naha, the capital of Okinawa, where you can discover the lively Kokusai Dori (International Street) and the famed Shuri Castle.
- Take a day excursion to Kudaka Island, also referred to as the "Island of the Gods," to see the revered Kudaka Shrine.
- Explore the magnificent beaches on Ishigaki Island, including Kabira Bay and Yonehara Beach.

- Explore the region's spectacular coral reefs and marine life by diving or snorkeling in the area's pristine seas.

- Visit Taketomi Island by boat, which is renowned for its traditional Ryukyu village and stunning white sand beaches.

- Attending a traditional Eisa dance performance will allow you to experience the distinctive culture of the Okinawan people.

- Discover the Ishigaki Public Market to indulge in regional specialties and browse the gift stalls.

- Visit the picturesque Cape Hirakubozaki to cap off your journey, where you can take in the lighthouse and panoramic views.

7-Day Itinerary for First-Time Visitors

Day 1: Arrival in Tokyo - Fly into Haneda or Narita Airport in Tokyo - Be transferred to your hotel in the city's center - Wander the area near your hotel - Have dinner at a typical Japanese restaurant

Day 2: Tokyo Sightseeing - Begin the day by touring Senso-ji Temple and Nakamise Shopping Street in the famed Asakusa neighborhood. Take a boat tour down the Sumida River to take in the beautiful scenery.

Visit Meiji Shrine and Yoyogi Park for a tranquil escape in the center of the city. Explore the fashionable neighborhoods of Harajuku and Omotesando, famed for their fashion and shopping. Spend the evening in Shibuya, known for its busy intersection and exciting nightlife.

Day 3: Day Trip to Mount Fuji - Take an early train to Hakone, a picturesque town at the foot of Mount Fuji - Take in the breathtaking views of Mount Fuji from Lake Ashi or the Hakone Ropeway - Visit the Hakone Open-Air Museum for a special outdoor art experience - Unwind in the area's famous hot springs (onsen) - Return to Tokyo in the evening

Day 4: Kyoto - From Tokyo, take a bullet train to Kyoto. Explore Kinkaku-ji Temple (Golden Pavilion) and take in the tranquil gardens.

Visit the renowned Fushimi Inari Shrine and stroll through its thousands of iconic red torii gates. Explore the historic Gion district, known for its traditional wooden houses and geisha culture. Take a stroll along the Philosopher's Path, a picturesque trail lined with cherry blossoms (if visiting during spring) or vibrant foliage (if visiting during autumn).

- In a Kyoto restaurant, take pleasure in a classic kaiseki (multi-course) supper.

Day 5: Nara Day Trip - Spend the day in Nara, a city famous for its friendly deer and ancient temples, and then return to Kyoto in the evening. While there, you'll visit Todai-ji Temple, which is home to the Great Buddha statue, explore Nara Park, where you can interact with the park's tame deer, who roam freely, and Kasuga Taisha Shrine.

Day 6: Hiroshima and Miyajima Island - Take the bullet train from Kyoto to Hiroshima - Explore the Itsukushima Shrine and hike up Mount Misen for panoramic views - Learn about the World War II atomic bombing at the Hiroshima Peace Memorial Park and Museum - Take a ferry to Miyajima Island -

- Have lunch with delicious local seafood - return in the evening to Kyoto

Day 7: Osaka Take a day trip to Osaka, which is renowned for its lively food scene and energetic atmosphere; explore Osaka Castle, a historical site with lovely gardens; discover Dotonbori, the city's entertainment district, which is known for its street food and vibrant neon lights; try okonomiyaki, one of Osaka's well-known delicacies; and visit the Umeda Sky Building for panoramic views of the area. Depending on your arrangements for departure, return in the evening to Kyoto or Tokyo.

10-Day Itinerary for Cultural Enthusiasts

Day 1: Arrival in Paris, France - Tour the city's well-known attractions, including the Eiffel Tower, the Louvre Museum, and Notre Dame Cathedral - Visit Montmartre and Le Marais, two quaint areas, while taking a stroll along the Seine River.

Day 2: Vienna, Austria - See the magnificent Schönbrunn Palace and stroll through its immaculate grounds.
- Attend a classical music performance at one of Vienna's renowned concert venues and learn about the city's rich history and culture at the Hofburg Palace and Vienna State Opera.

Prague, Czech Republic, Day 3
- Explore the Old Town of Prague's cobblestone streets while admiring the Gothic design of the Prague Castle. Explore the Jewish Quarter to learn

about Prague's Jewish legacy and visit the famed Charles Bridge to enjoy the city's panoramic vistas.

Barcelona, Spain, Day 4 Admire Antoni Gaud's architectural marvels, such as the Sagrada Familia and Park Güell
- Visit the fashionable stores and art galleries in the thriving neighborhoods of El Raval and El Born - Dine on authentic Catalan food at a neighborhood tapas bar

Day 5: Kyoto, Japan - Experience the culture of Japan by touring historic temples including Kinkaku-ji (Golden Pavilion) and Kiyomizu-dera.
- Participate in a traditional tea ceremony to learn about the art of preparing tea; - Wander through Gion's ancient area in the hopes of spotting a geisha;

Day 6: Rome, Italy - Learn about ancient Roman history by visiting the Colosseum and the Roman Forum - Explore the Vatican City and be amazed by the Sistine Chapel and St. Peter's Basilica - Go on a culinary tour and savor delectable Italian cuisine

Day 7: Istanbul, Turkey - Visit the Blue Mosque and Hagia Sophia to learn more about Istanbul's rich cultural heritage.
- Explore the bustling Grand Bazaar to find authentic Turkish goods and spices.
- Take a leisurely sail along the Bosphorus Strait to take in the city's stunning scenery.

Day 8: Cairo, Egypt - Explore the historic pyramids of Giza and the Sphinx - Go to the Egyptian Museum to witness the renowned Tutankhamun artifacts - Go on a Nile River cruise to take in the local music and dancing of Egypt

Day 9: India's Delhi
Explore Old Delhi and stop at historical sites like the Red Fort and Jama Masjid. Ride a rickshaw through Chandni Chowk's busy lanes and sample the local cuisine.

- To understand about Delhi's Mughal past, visit the famous Qutub Minar and Humayun's Tomb.

Marrakech, Morocco, Day 10 Explore the lively souks and get lost in Medina's twisting streets - View the stunning architecture and gardens of the Bahia Palace and the Jardin Majorelle - Try a tagine dish and a cup of mint tea to experience traditional Moroccan cuisine.

14-Day Itinerary for Nature Lovers

Day 1: Japan - When you go to Tokyo, choose a place to stay and settle in.
- Discover the zoo, museums, and expansive Ueno Park, a park in the center of the city famous for its stunning cherry blossoms in the spring.
- Visit Shibuya's Meiji Shrine, a tranquil haven amid the busy city.

Day 2: Day trip to Mount Fuji - Enjoy the breathtaking views of the summit from the beaches of Lake Kawaguchi on a day trip to Mount Fuji, Japan's highest mountain and a UNESCO World Heritage Site. Visit Mount Fuji's 5th Station on a guided trek (if the weather permits).

Day 3: Nikko - Visit Nikko, a small town renowned for its magnificent shrines and scenic surroundings. Visit Toshogu Shrine, a UNESCO World Heritage Site that is embellished with elaborate wood carvings. Discover the breathtaking Nikko National Park, which features waterfalls, lakes, and beautiful hiking trails.

Day 4: Hakone - Travel to this well-known hot spring resort town by beautiful train and cable car. Go to Owakudani, a volcanic valley with sulfur eruptions and hot springs. On a clear day, take a boat trip on Lake Ashi to take in the breathtaking vistas of Mount Fuji.

Travel to Kamikochi, a charming highland region in the Japanese Alps, on the fifth day.

- Take in the spectacular views of the surrounding peaks while hiking along the Azusa River.

- Visit the Taisho Pond to contemplate its serene beauty.

Day 6: Kyoto - Travel by bullet train to Kyoto, the nation's cultural center, and take a calm stroll through the imposing bamboo grove at Arashiyama.

- Visit the renowned UNESCO World Heritage Site Kiyomizu-Dera Temple, which offers breathtaking views of the city.

Day 7: Nara - Go on a day tour of this city, which is renowned for its amiable deer and historic temples. Visit Todai-ji Temple, which has the largest bronze Buddha figure in the world. Explore Nara Park and get up close and personal with the roaming deer.

Day 8: Miyajima - Visit Itsukushima Shrine, one of Japan's most recognizable attractions, while on the island of Miyajima.

- Take a hike up Mount Misen to get a bird's-eye perspective of the island. Try regional specialties like grilled oysters and Momiji Manju (cakes in the shape of an apple).

Day 9: Hiroshima - Spend the day in Hiroshima and visit the Peace Memorial Park and Museum, which is devoted to fostering peace and honoring the atomic bomb victims. Discover the island of Miyajima and its renowned floating torii gate.

Day 10: Takayama - Visit Takayama, a historic city renowned for its festivals and meticulously preserved traditional architecture.
- Visit the Takayama Jinya, a historic government building, and meander through the Old Town. Discover the thatched-roof cottages of the Hida Folk Village, an outdoor museum.

Day 11: Shirakawa-go - Spend the day in Shirakawa-go, which is home to the traditional

Gassho-Zukuri farmhouses and is a UNESCO World Heritage Site.

- Investigate the community and discover the distinctive design of these steep-roofed homes.

Day 12: Kanazawa - Visit Kanazawa, a city renowned for its beautifully maintained Edo-era neighborhoods and gardens.

- One of Japan's most renowned gardens is the Kenroku-en Garden.

- Discover the Higashi Chaya District and take in geisha shows and traditional tea houses.

Day 13: Hakodate - Travel by bullet train to this city on Hokkaido Island's southernmost point, Hakodate. View the city and the surrounding shoreline from Mount Hakodate while there. Visit the old churches and Western-style structures in the Motomachi District.

Day 14: Sapporo - Arrive in Hokkaido's capital city of Sapporo.

- Take a tour of Odori Park, a sizable park in the heart of the city famous for its lovely flowers and seasonal festivities.

- Discover the background of Japanese beer brewing at the Sapporo Beer Museum.

- Visit a nearby fish market like Nijo Market or Curb Market for a delectable dinner.

With this 14-day tour, nature lovers may explore Japan's rich cultural heritage in places like Tokyo, Kyoto, and Hiroshima in addition to its breathtaking natural beauty. This tour offers the ideal fusion of nature, history, and adventure, from the renowned Mount Fuji to the serene shrines and quaint villages.

Customizable Itineraries for Different Interests

1. A typical itinerary in Japan would look something like this:

-Day 1: Arrive in Tokyo and explore Asakusa, a historic district that is home to the renowned

Senso-ji Temple and Nakamise Shopping Street. Visit Hamarikyu Gardens' traditional garden.

- Day 2: Spend the day in Kyoto, where you may see famous sites including Arashiyama Bamboo Grove, Fushimi Inari Shrine, and Kinkaku-ji (Golden Pavilion).

- Day 3: Visit Todai-ji Temple, which houses the biggest bronze Buddha statue in Japan, and learn about the historic city of Nara. Explore the deer park and stroll through Naramachi's historic streets.

- Day 4: Travel back to Tokyo and discover Kamakura, a historic area renowned for its stunning temples and shrines, including the Great Buddha of Kamakura.

Take a gorgeous boat trip on Lake Ashi on Day 5 and visit the historic hot spring town of Hakone. Take in Mount Fuji's 360-degree vistas from the Hakone Ropeway.

Explore the historical village of Takayama in the Japanese Alps on day six. Explore the old merchant homes in the Sanmachi Suji neighborhood and unwind in the nearby hot springs.

- Day 7: Visit the Kenroku-en Garden, one of Japan's most stunning gardens, while in the ancient city of Kanazawa. Discover the district of Higashi Chaya, famous for its old-fashioned tea establishments.

- Day 8: Fly back to Tokyo and tour the historic Yanaka district. Visit the ancient temples and shrines while meandering through the confined alleyways.

- Day 9: Spend the day in the picturesque town of Nikko and explore the UNESCO World Heritage site known as Toshogu Shrine. Discover the natural splendor of Nikko National Park. - On day 10, go sightseeing in Kyoto's Gion neighborhood and take in a traditional Geisha performance. Explore the lovely Kiyomizu-dera Temple and take a stroll through the winding lanes lined with Machiya cottages.

2. Outdoor activities in nature Itinerary: - Day 1: Fly into Tokyo and spend the day exploring the

bustling metropolis. Take a stroll through Shinjuku Gyoen National Garden and Ueno Park.

- Day 2: Fly to Hokkaido, where you can go hiking in Daisetsuzan National Park. Enjoy a hike, look for wildlife, and unwind in a natural hot spring.

- Day 3: Visit Kamikochi, a lovely mountain region famous for its hiking paths and breathtaking scenery, in the Japanese Alps.

Day 4: Travel to Shirakawa-go, a traditional village renowned for its distinctive thatched-roof homes, a UNESCO World Heritage site. Enjoy the natural beauty and discover the culture of the area.

Visit Mount Aso, an active volcano in Kumamoto, on Day 5. A trip to the crater will reward you with breathtaking scenery.

- Day 6: Take a tour of the island of Yakushima, which is renowned for its ancient cedar trees and hiking paths. Visit Yakusugi Land, a UNESCO World Heritage Site, and unwind in the natural hot springs.

- Day 7: Fly to Okinawa, where you can take advantage of the island's pristine beaches and waterways. Take a boat cruise to see the nearby islands and snorkel or dive in the coral reefs.

- Day 8: Travel to the lovely island of Miyajima, which is close to Hiroshima. Visit Itsukushima Shrine, famous for its characteristic floating torii gate, and climb Mount Misen for panoramic views.

- Day 9: Visit the isolated island of Rebun in the north and explore its hiking paths and distinctive alpine flora. Enjoy the peace of the island and travel to the beautiful Cape Sukoton.

Return to Tokyo on Day 10 and explore the beautiful grounds of Shinjuku Gyoen National Garden or wander along the Meguro River, which is adorned with cherry blossom trees in the spring.

3. Food & Culinary Itinerary:

- Day 1: Fly into Tokyo and start your culinary journey in the humming Tsukiji Fish Market. Eat some delicious fish and fresh sushi.

Day 2: Go on an Osaka culinary tour and sample some of the city's street fare, including takoyaki, okonomiyaki, and kishka Tsu. Visit the thriving food district of Dotonbori.

- On the third day, go to Kyoto and take part in a ceremonial tea ceremony. Learn about the regional ingredients used in Japanese cuisine by visiting Nishiki Market.

- Day 4: Visit Hiroshima and sample the renowned okonomiyaki made in Hiroshima. Visit a local sake brewery before going to the Hondori Shopping Arcade.

- Day 5: Take in Fukuoka's culinary scene, which is renowned for its delectable ramen and street cuisine. Visit Nakasu's renowned Yatai food stands.

Day 6: Go to the seaside town of Kanazawa and sample some of the local seafood specialties, including snow crab and sea urchin. Learn about the local ingredients used in traditional Kanazawa cuisine by exploring the Omicho Market.

4. Adventure & Outdoor Itinerary:

- Day 1: Fly into Tokyo and hike Mount Takao, which provides sweeping views of the city. As an alternative, consider indoor bouldering at a city climbing gym.

- Day 2: Go skiing or snowboarding in the well-known ski resorts of Hakuba or Nozawa Onsen in Nagano.

Travel to Hiroshima and board a ferry to Miyajima Island on the third day. For spectacular views of the Seto Inland Sea surrounding you, climb Mount Misen.

Visit Yakushima Island on Day 4, which is home to ancient cedar trees and hiking paths and is a World Heritage Site. Trek to the 7,000-year-old cedar tree Jomon Sugi.

- On the fifth day, trek the Nakasendo Trail while exploring the Japanese Alps in Nagano. Visit ancient post towns and enjoy the beautiful alpine scenery.

- Day 6: Visit Hokkaido's Shiretoko National Park to enjoy wildlife viewing. Visit seals, brown bears, and eagles in the wild by taking a boat excursion.

Conclusion

In conclusion, the number one place on every traveler's list for 2023 should be Japan. The nation provides the ideal fusion of traditional and modern elements, enabling visitors to take in the country's rich cultural past while also taking advantage of modern conveniences. The natural beauty of Japan is extremely enchanting, from the magnificent cherry blossoms in the spring to the bright fall foliage. Japan presents a variety of options for exploration and adventure with its delicious cuisine, magnificent landscapes, and distinctive cultural experiences. Japan has everything, whether you're interested in exploring historic temples and castles, cutting-edge technology and shopping, or getting to know the local traditions and customs. Therefore, be sure to schedule your vacation to Japan for 2023 and prepare for an extraordinary voyage of discovery.

Printed in Great Britain
by Amazon

27158665R00145